NIELS VANDECASTEELE
STEFAN DOUTRELUINGNE

Create your own
SUPERFANS

MAKE A
DIFFERENCE
WITH AMBASSADOR
MARKETING!

Lannoo
Campus

D/2021/45/265 – ISBN 978 94 014 8270 7 – NUR 802

| COVER LAYOUT | Best Advice.be |
| INTERIOR LAYOUT | Banananas.net |

© Niels Vandecasteele, Stefan Doutreluingne & Uitgeverij Lannoo nv, Tielt, 2021.

Uitgeverij LannooCampus is part of Lannoo Uitgeverij, the book and multimedia division of Uitgeverij Lannoo nv.

Uitgeverij LannooCampus
Vaartkom 41 bus 01.02   PO Box 23202
3000 Leuven   1100 DS Amsterdam
Belgium   The Netherlands
www.lannoocampus.com

CONTENTS

CHAPTER 3
THE SCIENCE OF RECOMMENDATIONS

CHAPTER 4
THE AMBASSADORS FOR YOUR COMPANY

CHAPTER 5
DEVELOPING YOUR AMBASSADOR MARKETING

CHAPTER 6
THE POWER OF MERCHANDISE

CONTENTS

INTRO

FOREWORD

According to the oft-cited quote by Pablo Picasso, the Talmud or Confucius (depending on the source you consult), there are three things that a real man must do during his life: plant a tree, have a child and write a book. As I already have a large garden and four daughters, I had no hesitation in jumping on board when the plans for writing this book emerged over a long lunch. Niels and I regularly have lunches together, to keep abreast of each other's life, career and business opportunities. Although there is a significant age difference between us (I am old enough to be Niels' father), our paths have crossed regularly in recent years. It was my friend John who first introduced me to his ambitious nephew, with the request to have a look at some of his (business) ideas and to test them against my marketing experience. We clicked immediately and since then we have never lost touch. We meet frequently to exchange thoughts on new business trends and the opportunities they present. Niels' youthful enthusiasm and entrepreneurial spirit perfectly complement my more strategic and creative approach to marketing and communication. Readers will discover more about this mix later in the book, where a number of practical cases and examples from Niels' activities are supplemented with strategic models that have been verified against my more than 30 years of professional experience in the communications world. Our joint insights have been brought together in *Create Your Own Superfans*, in which we want to share our knowledge with our readers through a hybrid combination of theory and practice. Anyone who works professionally in the field of communication knows that nothing beats word of mouth. When you are 'taken with' something or someone, you just can't help talking about it. It is this kind of ambassadorship and fandom that forms the core of this book. So spread the word!

Stefan

OPPORTUNITY KNOCKS...

24 April 2020. The world has been at a standstill for more than a month. COVID-19 has normal daily life firmly in its suffocating grip and the Belgian government has announced drastic measures to try to limit its effects, including the wearing of face masks. At Merchandise Essentials, normal business activity has also ground to a halt. Team building, trade fairs and events are all being cancelled wholesale, accompanied by a logical slump in the demand for personalised clothing. Within a matter of days, we see all our potential deals for the months ahead go up in smoke and even the deals that have already been finalised are annulled or put on hold. To cut a long story short: this is an unforeseen disaster that could have catastrophic consequences for our company. The support measures introduced by the government allow us to send our staff home on semi-paid leave. After that, all we can do is sit tight and wait until the storm passes...

Or that, at least, was the plan until that fateful twenty-fourth of April. We had seen an increasing number of signs in pharmacies that their supplies of face masks had run out and that they had no idea when new stock would be received. Following an earlier rush to stockpile toilet paper, it seemed that face masks were now the next target for panic buying. We immediately understood that the demand for these masks would shoot through the ceiling in the weeks and months ahead. If companies wanted to restart their operations in the near future, it was certain that for safety reasons the wearing of face masks by all their employees would be the only option. In fact, it would probably be compulsory. Daniel, our Polish production manager, and Steven, my co-founder, soon saw the opportunity that this could offer. In the past, we had already carried out research into the possibilities presented by personalised face masks, basing our study on trends in Asia, where face masks have long been part of many people's personal outfit.

Steven and Daniel moved into overdrive. Within 24 hours, Daniel had convinced one of our production partners to re-open his factory for the production of a number of prototypes. At the same time, our sales teams hit the streets to visit hundreds of pharmacies one by one to propose our new masks as the answer to their supply shortage. The result was a chain reaction on a scale that we will probably never experience again. The first orders came in almost at once: 50 masks, 100 masks, 200 masks... Every pharmacy we visited placed small test orders, partly out of curiosity, partly as a back-up in case their usual suppliers failed to deliver. Production manager Daniel persuaded our producer to start larger scale production of the prototypes with a small team. This was by no means easy, since at that time almost every textile factory in Poland had shut down as a consequence of the near total collapse of the retail sector.

Day after day, we continued to get more and more orders. And once we had made our first deliveries to the pharmacies, the news of our products spread like wildfire. Our first customers were quick to recommend our masks to all their fellow pharmacists. What's more, the orders of these new customers kept on getting bigger and bigger. In this way, we were quickly able to grow to a demand level of thousands of masks per day, but even then it didn't stop. Fully in line with the raison d'être and philosophy of our company, we started to make personalised masks that matched the house style of the ordering companies, which by now were no longer confined to the pharmaceutical sector alone. This was a key part of the motivation behind our initial thinking: if companies were investing heavily in face masks, this would mean that individual citizens and the government would no longer need to do the same. And as far as the companies were concerned, their personalised masks were a great source of positive publicity. It soon became clear that this was the key factor in what was quickly becoming a massive success story. Our sales shot through the ten thousand masks per day mark and just kept on rising. Every time we opened our mailbox, dozens of new orders were waiting to be processed. To meet this demand, our production team was now working day and night.

'I saw the masks you made for X and would like to order something similar for our company.' 'A fellow contractor at Y told me that you can make certified and personalised masks and I am interested is something like that for our people.' These were the comments that we continued to hear day after day. The only reason why our masks become so amazingly popular in such a short space of time was that news about them was spread by word of mouth. Coupled with the willingness of our mask ambassadors to recommend our product to new customers, this resulted in an exponential rate of growth, which at its peak in early May 2020 reached more than one million masks sold per day! Such is the power of word-of-mouth advertising.

Of course, that is only one side of the story. Everything that is sold first needs to be made. If we at Merchandise Essentials sometimes felt as though we had been catapulted back to the Wild West, the feeling for our colleagues in Poland must have been ten times worse! On 24 April, Daniel phoned us to announce proudly that he had been able to boost production capacity from 1,000 to 5,000 masks per day, a massive increase of 500 percent. This was incredible, but it was not enough. We continued to pester him daily with the same single request: more capacity, please! As the pandemic grew, the pressure on us to deliver our masks as quickly as possible became ever greater. Everyone wanted them yesterday, or even sooner. To complicate things still further, we were taking in new orders at a rate of more than 10,000 per day, which was more than twice our existing level of production capacity. You didn't need to be a business genius to work out that at this pace we were digging our own grave.

It was during this crucial period that Daniel was able to pull off one of the finest examples of ambassador marketing that I have ever seen. To give you some idea of the scale of the challenge facing him, you first need to know something about the nature of the textile production landscape in Poland. The Poles have been making clothing for over a century and at one time the country was the largest textile producer in the world. During the 1990s, they made a huge breakthrough into the Russian market, where business is largely based on personal trust and confidence: the 'birds of a feather' principle. This means that it is not possible simply to contact a Polish textile factory and ask to become a customer. The entire industry is characterised by a closed and defensive attitude, especially towards unknown 'outsiders'. Outsiders like Merchandise Essentials. In short, we knew that there was no easy way to find new manufacturers who could scale up the production capacity for our face masks.

To make matters even worse, at the start of April 2020 the Polish textile market was flooded with requests from French and German companies who wanted to produce super-cheap (but largely sub-standard) masks at high speed, in the hope of making a quick killing from the crisis. This combination of increased competition for production capacity and a closed-minded production network that was wary of foreigners led to a rapid rise in the production cost for face masks. We also found ourselves engaging almost blindly in this price war, until one day Daniel gave us a much needed wake-up call: 'Listen guys, if we keep on agreeing with these destructive price rises, they will squeeze us for every last penny. I have an alternative plan that might work. If you trust me, I think I can increase capacity at a much lower cost.'

He did indeed have a plan – and it was as powerful as it was simple. He contacted all the producers with whom he (and, through him, Merchandise Essentials) had built up a good working relationship to ask which of their fellow producers they could suggest who might be interested in a longer-term collaboration. In this way, he was able to make use of our current ambassadors to secure introductions to potential new partners. In other words, we were no longer looking exclusively for producers who could help us to overcome the effects of the crisis in the short term, but for lasting and sustainable partnerships that would continue once the peak demand of the crisis had passed. It helped that our current production partners were satisfied both with our business dealings and with the constant stream of orders that we were able to supply, which is in contrast with the seasonal nature of the fashion industry.

Daniel's success in actively converting our existing suppliers into ambassadors gave us access to a previously untapped and largely unknown network of reliable producers. He was able to transform the mutual trust of companies that had known each other for decades into a unique advantage for Merchandise Essentials. And because we were offering long-term relationships instead of short-term opportunities, we were even able to convince our new partners to give us correct prices for the manufacture of our face masks. This smart strategy made it possible for us to increase the number of full-time seamstresses working for us from five to four hundred in just a few days! This was a remarkable achievement, but it would not have been possible without the stable relationships of trust that existed between all the parties concerned.

Eight weeks and three million face masks later, the level of demand collapsed almost as quickly as it had arisen. The orders dried up and the pressure on production capacity fell. It was only when the dust had finally settled that we were able to realise just how hard we had all worked and just how much we had been able to achieve together. On both the sales and the production side of our operations, we had taken huge strides forward in a remarkably short period of time. In the following weeks, one thing above all became clear to me: our success would not have been possible by relying exclusively on strategy, processes and stacks of money. It had been made possible by people and, more specifically, by the trust that people had in each other. That was the crucial factor that made everyone willing to put their reputations on the line for the sake of helping our company during those crazy face mask weeks in 2020. It was an unbelievable experience, and one that inspired me with the idea of writing this book and sharing the secret of our success with you. Because I am going to explain how you, too, can recruit an army of ambassadors to promote and support your company.

In this book you will learn everything about the power of ambassador marketing and how it can be used to boost your brand. Not only will I lead you through the necessary theory, but will also provide you with concrete tools and techniques that will allow you to start building up your own ambassador network with a minimum of delay. Because that is one of the biggest advantages of using ambassadors: they generate positive results very quickly. Before you know it, you will have more leads than ever before – and that can only be good for your business, can't it?

Enjoy your reading!

Niels

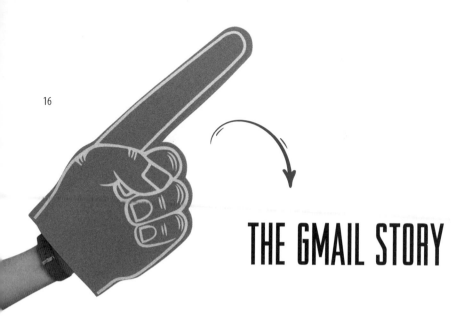

THE GMAIL STORY

Everyone knows Gmail: worldwide, more than 425 million people make use of Google's web-based e-mail service. Gmail is famed for its user-friendliness and its intuitive interface. Hardly surprising, then, that its popularity grew so rapidly after its launch. Or so you might think.

What is less well known is that without one of the most successful word-of-mouth marketing campaigns in history Gmail might never have made it off the ground.

Gmail actually started as a closed e-mail system for Google employees. Its launch for public use in April 2004 was very low key. Google did little more than encourage its employees to send as many invitations as they could to family and friends, asking them to join the beta test version of Gmail. Slowly but surely, these invitees were given the opportunity to send out new invitations to family and friends of their own. In this way, Gmail evolved from an exclusive network of people who all knew each other into an international phenomenon that today connects millions of people.

This underlines the super-power of ambassadorship, particularly when you bear in mind that none of the people invited had any real need of Gmail, since they were already using some other perfectly acceptable mailing service. By focusing fully on recommendations to family and friends, rather than pushing the service and its possibilities via traditional advertising channels, Google was able to convince.

millions of people to support their product, even though they didn't need it! The company used word-of-mouth marketing to disseminate information about Gmail through thousands of existing mini-networks. The campaign continued to spread like an oil slick, thanks to the possibility given to existing users to invite new users to join the Gmail club. This was pure member-get-member marketing of a kind that is still used today; for example, by companies like Hello Fresh. They give their subscribers free meal boxes or discounts that can be gifted to potential new customers, so that these people can test the Hello Fresh concept for themselves.

The principles of ambassador marking are not particularly complicated and if you apply them correctly and consistently they are almost always successful. Very successful.

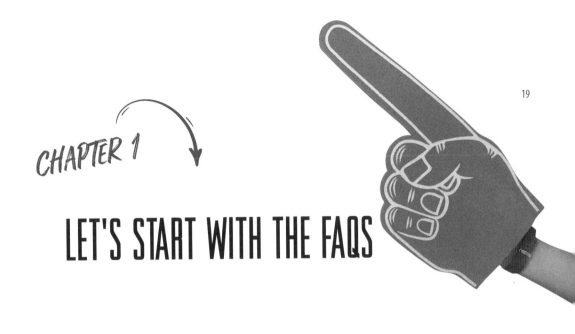

CHAPTER 1

LET'S START WITH THE FAQS

*'Part of being successful is about asking questions
and listening to the answers.'*

WHAT IS AMBASSADOR MARKETING?

What do Club Brugge (or any other football club), Channel Zero and Christianity have in common? All three can count on the support of a loyal group of fans who display a high level of emotional commitment. That is what being a fan means: you have an emotional connection with the object of your fascination and/or affection. Real fans will go through hell and high water to support their 'idols' (club, group, city, company, product, etc.) and will defend them in all circumstances, even if this is sometimes against their better judgement. As a result, they are often prepared to associate openly with the focus of their idolatry. What's more, this is not an objective choice, based on a rational analysis. One of the things that is most likely to determine your fandom is your environment and your peers. In Niels' family, for example, everyone is a fan of Club Brugge and has been for generations. It is something that you are fed from birth, almost as a kind of indoctrination. Little wonder, then, that Niels is now also a fervent Club supporter. Because he grew up surrounded by this passion in others, it is still very much alive and kicking in him! Niels backs 'his' team unconditionally, in good times and bad.

In our contacts with other entrepreneurs, the importance of fans and ambassadors is a frequent subject of discussion. But whenever we start to explore how their staff and customers can be converted into ambassadors, a number of counter-arguments soon begin to emerge: 'That won't work in our case, because our brand isn't really cool' (see below) or 'We are hardly the hippest company in our sector, so how do we expect people to get excited enough about us to become a fan?' This is, of course, a good question, but finding the right answer will open up new perspectives and make it possible for your playing field to be significantly enlarged. Niels' answer is often something like this: 'Being a fan is all about emotion. It is not a decision based on a careful weighing of the facts. If people could only become fans of the best, the strongest or the prettiest, we would all end up being supporters of the same brands and teams. In the world of sport, everyone would be a fan of the top team. The teams lower down in the pecking order would have no supporters at all, but we all know that this is not what happens. For example, people often like to support the underdogs, simply because they are underdogs. Likewise, we sometimes become fans of a particular club because that is where we were born or how we were brought up. Or sometimes because the exploits of a particular team have managed to touch us in some way. You can become a fan of something for no better reason than all your friends are a fan of that thing. In my case, I am a Club Brugge fan because my dad and the rest of my family have been fans for years. And it is the same with a company or a business venture: you have the potential to reach people and to move them emotionally. Of course, at an intrinsic level this means that you will probably not only have fans, but also opponents. But that doesn't matter. You might think that you are the most boring company in your sector, but even if this is true it will not necessarily prevent you from acquiring a fan base. Irrespective of your drab self-image, your employees and your loyal customers still have a genuine connection with your brand. Okay, having a strong and cool brand obviously helps, but it is by no means a prerequisite for building up an army of enthusiastic fans.'

WHEN IS A BRAND 'COOL'?

Joeri van den Bergh and Mattias Behrer, who are research specialists in the field of youth marketing, make a distinction between three important aspects of 'coolness': originality, popularity and attractiveness.[1] According to Eurib, the no.1 knowledge platform for brand management, design management and reputation management, a brand can be experienced as iconic if it has a high 'cool' factor. Harley-Davidson, Nike and Apple owe their status as 'best global brand' to their cool image.

But what exactly is it that makes consumers experience a brand or product as being cool? Researchers have investigated this key question in depth and have come to the conclusion that the concept of autonomy plays a crucial role. They are also clear on another crucial point: regarding something as cool is not the same as regarding it as fun. Yet beyond this, the experts are still finding it difficult to agree on an exact and generally accepted definition of coolness. Amongst other things, this means that it is not easy for brands that focus on a mass market to build up and cultivate a cool image. If everyone thinks you are cool, you lose the exclusiveness that is part of the essence of coolness. Similarly, it is impossible to be cool for every consumer at the same time: your more autonomously-minded customers will never want to belong to the same group as your 'average' customers. In other words, there are different kinds of coolness.

Perhaps the results of all this coolness research can be more easily and more usefully applied in the public arena than in the world of business. For example, governments have been trying for years to change the behaviour of consumers (initially young people, but nowadays increasingly generation X-ers and boomers) through anti-smoking and anti-alcohol campaigns. These campaigns mainly emphasise that smoking and drinking are bad for you. However, this usually has little effect, because it is the very fact of deviating from the (health) norm that most young people find 'cool' about cigarettes and booze. According to Warren and Campbell[2] it would therefore be smarter to label this high-risk behaviour as mainstream or conformist, so that it would appear to be less cool!

FAN OR AMBASSADOR? DIFFERENT SCENTS OF THE SAME PERFUME

At heart, fans and ambassadors are essentially the same. The biggest differ-ence between a fan and an ambassador is how they give outward expression to their fandom. A fan can do this in the peace and seclusion of his own home, where no one needs to see him except those in his immediate circle. Even when they pursue their passion in public, many sports fans and music fans do not feel the need to get dressed up in the recognisable symbols of their fandom, such as the scarf of their favourite football team or the t-shirt of their favourite pop star. They enjoy being a fan in the privacy of their own thoughts and emotions.

When a fan starts to talk about you actively and seeks to involve others in his fan experience, this is when he becomes an ambassador. He is enthusi-astic about how much fun it is to work for you or how happy he is to collab-orate with your company. Ambassadors are fans who are prepared to put their own reputation on the line in order to push you forward into the lime-light. An ambassador is so satisfied and so strongly convinced by what you represent that he wants to make a personal contribution to help you grow.

In this book we will look at different ways that will allow you to convert fans into true ambassadors, so that even more people will be attracted to your company. In short, we will show you how to turn these ambassadors into your most powerful sales and marketing channel.

IN THE BEGINNING ... THE BIRTH OF MERCHANDISE ESSENTIALS

The story of Steven Callens and Niels Vandecasteele starts in 2013. Mer-chandise Essentials (then still Night Essentials) was founded on the basis of their own experience of 'being a fan and having fans'. At that time, Steven

Steven Deejay
© CDR – HLN – DPG media 28052014

was still building a successful career as DJ Audiophonic. His days and nights were filled with performances at top national and international festivals. Steven was a DJ pur sang, with an unconditional love of music. He also knew exactly what it takes to whip a crowd into a frenzy. However, to make the breakthrough as a DJ, it is essential to be able to guarantee an event organiser the presence of a certain kind of public (in other words, a fan base). Understandably, they prefer to book artists who are likely to attract the largest number of people. For a DJ, the best way to build up your own audience is to have your own music. Having your own music helps you to develop a real fan base. If you are fortunate enough to score a hit, the number of your bookings will grow exponentially. But Steven's real passion lay in a different direction. He was not really interested in making and producing his own music. Instead, he saw himself more as a kind of master of ceremonies, who could excite the emotions of a large group of people. This presented him with a serious challenge: how could he find another way to build up a large group of fans without making music himself? Social media offered various possibilities in terms of communication, but he decided to focus his attention primarily on the intensive merchandising of his act, so that his fans would be clearly identifiable at the festivals where he played. This made his brand stronger, which in turn meant that the festivals wanted to book him more often. As a result, Steven became increasingly aware of the power of merchandising.

Niels' passion for merchandising grew from being a fan himself. He was not only a fan of Steven's Audiophonic, but also (and primarily) of the late DJ Avicii. Niels followed Avicii from the start of his career and when his idol was programmed to appear at Tomorrowland in 2012 Niels knew that this was an opportunity too good to miss: he would finally get to see the man himself in action. He not only bought a ticket for the festival but also decided that for the first time he would buy an artist's merchandise. To understand what followed, you need to know something about Avicii's popularity at that time. The DJ Mag Top 100 (the annual world chart of DJs) had him listed in third place, amongst all the other DJ greats of the day (Armand van Buuren, Tiësto, David Guetta, etc.). He had millions of fans on Facebook and SoundCloud. Imagine Niels' surprise when he discovered that this megastar had no merchandising products of his own! It was impossible for him to give expression to his fandom by buying a t-shirt or a baseball cap, because these things simply did not exist. This, thought Niels, was a ridiculous situation. Every self-respecting rock band with just a handful of fans had its own merchandising, but here was an artist of world stature with nothing at all! His curiosity stimulated by this fact, Niels decided to look into the matter. He went through the entire *DJ Mag* Top 100 list to see how many nightlife artists sold merchandising products. He was amazed to discover that the answer was less than a quarter: 76 of the top 100 artists had no products that they could offer to their millions of fans. Incomprehensible! Absurd! Niels immediately began to sense a real opportunity: in his opinion, there was certainly more than enough demand in the market.

A short time later, Niels and Steven had a meeting in a café in the West Flanders town of Roeselare. Niels wanted to pitch his idea to Steven; namely, to expand what Steven was already doing for himself as a DJ and extend it to all his other DJ colleagues. In this way, their fans would eventually become ambassadors, who in turn would attract even more new fans.

Like Niels, Steven was quick to see the possibilities this offered and agreed to back the plan. And so Marketing Essentials was born. You could say that the company's foundation reflects both sides of the same coin. Steven wanted to expand his fan base and transform them into ambassadors through merchandising, while Niels wanted to show the world that he was an Avicii fan. Today, Merchandise Essentials does exactly the same for other companies and brands. It ensures that fans become ambassadors by allowing them to demonstrate their pride and passion for the object of their fanship.

From Night Essentials to Sunday

During its history, our company has changed its name twice. The first time was much less drastic than the second time. At the very beginning, Steven and I were two very enthusiastic (and very inexperienced) young men who simply wanted to do something with and about our passion. Our first business idea was to focus on DJs and events in the nightlife scene. For this reason, we wanted to choose a name that linked well to the market in which we intended to operate. We eventually decided that Night Essentials seemed to fit the bill perfectly.

However, time passes and things change, especially in the world of business. We grew quickly, our team got bigger and bigger, and the nature of our customers began to diversify. The nightlife scene was now only a part of what we did, since we were already making collections for many different kinds of companies and clothing brands. In other words, Night Essentials no longer fully reflected our range of activities. What had been a strength in the beginning was now becoming a weakness. It frightened off companies that had no connection with nightlife or music.

In January 2016, we made our first visit to Poland in search of new production options. One evening in our hotel in Krakow, after a few too many Polish beers, we began to discuss the company name. We were both convinced that the 'Night' part of the name was holding us back, whereas the 'Essentials' part still fully represented the philosophy behind our business. After all, our product range was restricted to the basic necessities of merchandising. We didn't offer a 500-page catalogue full of worthless tat. We marketed a limited selection of top-quality goods. No half measures. Just essential premium merchandise. That evening, we decided to change the name to Merchandise Essentials. A name that we were proud to bear... until the summer of 2021.

Corona ensured that what had been an evolution in our business became a revolution. During 2020 and 2021 we worked enormously hard at Merchandise Essentials. We invested huge amounts of time and resources in the internal development of our team, new procedures, new strategy, new software, new customers... In just a year, merchandise Essentials had been transformed into a completely different company. Like a caterpillar emerging from its corona cocoon, we had developed with dazzling speed into a post-corona butterfly. We were no longer what we had once been. The only problem was that the outside world did not immediately recognise that this transformation had taken place. They still saw us as the same company as we had been 12 months earlier.

The time had come to say thank you and farewell to Merchandise Essentials. We needed to move forward under a new name. A name that would resonate with the companies with whom we work and reflect the philosophy we wish to embody. Right from the very start of our entrepreneurial adventure, we had always been convinced that people who wear your brand on a Sunday are people who are committed to you totally, who believe in you for the full 100 percent or more. No one but a true ambassador would wear your t-shirt to a Sunday barbecue with family and friends! And so we choose the name 'Sunday'. For us, it symbolises everything we do and why we do it. Sunday is here to stay.

Niels Vandecasteele

Summer 2021

THE IMPACT OF AMBASSADORS: FLUID KARMA

The story in the introduction and the anecdote about how our company got its most recent name are both telling illustrations of the power and impact of ambassadors. In our own company, we also continue to set a strong focus on the people in and around Sunday and seek ways to make them even more committed. That being said, it is important to realise that ambassadorship is not a strategy where you can press a button once each month and add another 1 percent to your return. It is more like a highly fluid form of karma. You know that you will receive back whatever you give (and more); the problem is that you never know when this is going to happen. By involving people actively in your company through merchandising, you indirectly make them a part of your team. It is like having an army of ambassadors encouraging you with great passion and fire from the stands of Wembley or the Bernabéu during the final of the Champions League. It is this encouragement, this passion and fire that inspires you and drives you forward to make one last supreme effort. Suddenly, you find a strength you never knew you had, rush into the box and smash home the winning goal in the 94th minute! You no longer expected to do it and you don't really know how you did it. But you do know that the people in the stands were a part of it.

Ambassador marketing demands a specific approach and a continuous focus from everyone in your organisation. As a business strategy, it is not only the responsibility of the marketing department, but of every department throughout the company. What's more, it is actually quite good fun! By focusing on the people in and around your company, you can succeed in uniting everyone around a single collective goal. Much has already been written about this in the professional literature, but in this book we will concentrate in particular on how you can secure people's engagement to share the philosophy you want them to share. How can you stimulate people to talk enthusiastically about you and your company? Ambassadors always have one or more elements in common. But the most important of these is their willingness to tell others about you and your products or services with passion. In short, they belong to your 'tribe'.

WHAT ARE TRIBES?

Viewed from an anthropological perspective, a tribe is a collection of individuals in a broadly like-minded group with a clear leader or some other unifying element. It is a social structure that embraces family, friends, acquaintances and others who share a common social, religious or economic bond. Perhaps they come from the same background. Or speak the same language. Or practise the same customs. Viewed in these terms, it is easy for all of us to imagine ways in which we can belong to a particular tribe or group.

Humans, it seems, are social creatures that (for better or worse) have a need to belong, to be part of a group, to seek out their peers. In *Sapiens* Yuval Noah Harari describes how the cognitive revolution made it possible for homo sapiens to collaborate in large groups through communication and the transfer of ideas and ideologies. This led to the creation of social groups that felt a sense of solidarity and connection. The formation of tribes in this manner has already inspired many marketing authors.

It is indisputable that in our modern world, which is so often dominated by the omnipresence of social media (Twitter, Facebook, WhatsApp, Instagram, etc.), it is easier than ever before to reach a large public. As a result, tribes have never developed as quickly as they are developing today. In the United States, for example, Trump supporters were united into a single group almost exclusively by social media. This immediately highlights another important characteristic of a tribe: they follow a leader or a shared guiding principle. Without a leader or leadership, there can be no tribe, just a loose collection of individuals.

In other words, the desire to be divided into tribes, to find a group to which we feel we can belong, is something quintessentially human. People have an inborn need to be part of something bigger than themselves, a hunger to feel connectedness with others and to experience the possibility of change for the better. It is a kind of survival mechanism: by being part of a tribe (The Blue Army of Club Brugge, grandparents against global warming, veganism, etc.) we contribute to our group, but in return we get information, friendship, good advice and a feeling of safety. People feel attracted to leaders and their ideas, and find it difficult to resist the impulse to belong to something new that offers the exciting prospect of movement and change.

Tribes thrive on belief, on deep personal conviction. Belief in an idea, a product, a person, a community: the possibilities are almost endless. Tribes are characterised by their great respect and admiration not only for whoever or whatever leads them, but also for other members of the tribe. Without a leader or a leading ideal, without a crucial connective factor, without communication and support, a tribe is just a meaningless mob.

CHAPTER 2

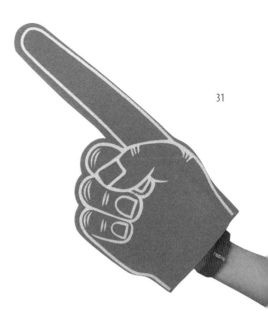

TRIBES & CIRCLES

'I am a sportsman, not a brand ambassador,
besides being the first goalkeeper of Adidas.'

Manuel Neuer

Ambassador marketing can seem highly organic and, as a result, highly complex. It is all about human interactions that often take place spontaneously. How on earth can you turn these interactions into a mathematical model that you can apply consistently? Short answer: you can't. Fortunately, a number of simplified presentations will allow you to understand precisely what ambassador marketing involves.

TRIBES IN THE 21ST CENTURY

We human beings are predestined to live in groups. As a species, we evolved and were able to survive by learning how to think and cooperate in such groups. Many recent studies have reached this same conclusion: homo sapiens had (and still has) a better chance of surviving in a group than alone in the wilderness. This natural process of evolution has resulted in us developing a number of characteristics that maximise our survival chances within the group.

For example, in his bestselling book *Influence*, Robert Cialdini cites the results of various scientific research studies into the different qualities of group thinking. The main conclusion? What the group does is good.

Similarly, in *Humankind. A Hopeful History* Rutger Bregman argues that homo sapiens (whom he refers to as 'homo puppy') was able to outlive homo neanderthalensis primarily because of its better developed social skills. Put simply, the fact that, as a species, we lived in greater connectedness with each other ultimately saved our skin (both literally and figuratively).

The origins of our social behaviour date back to the dawn of time and to the earliest beginnings of human history. When we wandered the savannah as nomadic tribes, it was crucial to listen to and learn from the other members of the tribe if you wanted to survive. Which berries were safe to eat and which ones were poisonous? The shared knowledge of the group protected the individual against making wrong decisions. If some of our primeval ancestors ever felt the urge to 'go it alone' outside the group, they were not likely to last for very long. You only need to eat the wrong berries once and there is more chance of hunting down a mammoth if there are fifty of you than if you are on your own… In other words, countless generations of evolution have built into our DNA the understanding that people who can best accommodate themselves to the needs and demands of the group have the best chance of survival.

In essence, this method of group thinking has changed very little over the millennia. Even though the world today is much safer than in primeval times, so that our life is no longer quite so dependent on group solidarity, the dynamic of our behaviour remains much the same as it was when we were hunter-gatherers roaming the plains of central Africa. We still live in tribes, even though this is no longer what we call them. And we still attach great importance to what other members of our group say, think and do. This explains why word-of-mouth advertising and, more specifically, ambassador marketing can still have a huge impact. If different people say something good (or bad) about a company, our natural group feeling will very often persuade us to follow that opinion when it comes to making our purchasing decision. This also explains why nowadays marketing departments worldwide devote so much time, attention and money to influencers. On social media, these influencers are hired by companies to praise certain products, services, locations, etc. They are the new way to conduct word-of-mouth marketing and their success has been conclusively proven in research. Even so, some studies[3] suggest that micro-influencers (who have 50 or so followers) have a much higher 'like' rate (up to eight times higher) than influencers with hundreds of thousands of followers. If you add to this the fact that the decisions of 80 percent of people are influenced by others in their immediate circle, it soon becomes clear that micro-influencers are a more effective way to get your message across. This is only logical: after all, these micro-influencers are generally people who we know and respect personally. If someone from our modern tribe makes a recommendation, we are strongly inclined to take account of what they say. Likewise, if a friend or a member of your family says something negative about a company, you will usually not be prepared to risk working with that company, even if your own opinion was initially positive. The psychological mechanisms that once prevented us from eating the wrong berries or hunting alone for mammoths still save us today from making the wrong purchasing decisions.

TRIBES AND CATEGORIES

On Monday morning at precisely 7 o'clock, Emma sets off on her electric bicycle to the environmental department in Roeselare, where she works. During this daily ride, she thinks about next month's school party, which she will be helping to organise: Emma is an active member of the parents committee. At the same time, she is thinking about the family's plans for the coming weekend. Her daughter is taking part in a judo competition, while at the same time her son is performing at the music school. Her husband, who is a keen cyclist, intends to train with his club for a few hours on Sunday morning. This is easy to combine with the weekly session Emma has booked with her labrador at the dog training school. Which reminds her that she still wants to ask a question about retrieving on the Facebook page for dog lovers.

Eric has been wanting to do something about his physical condition for quite some time. Since the children moved out, he has been devoting more and more time to his great passion: music. He also gives music lessons to beginners. Together with his wife, Eric has also discovered the delights of fine dining, as a result of which they now visit a new restaurant each week. In a Whatsapp group with friends, they discuss the various places where they have eaten. However, this new 'hobby' has also had an unfortunate effect on his weight. Ever since his dear wife made a friendly remark about his steadily growing paunch, Eric has been determined to exercise more and slim down. He will start soon, but not this weekend. Because number one on his agenda this weekend is the performance of his pupils at the music school.

Saturday arrives and so far everything is going according to plan. Emma has dropped her daughter off at the judo competition and is now on her way to the music school. Eric checks the planning with all the pupils and gets the stage ready for their performance. The proud parents are sitting in the auditorium. The children are waiting nervously backstage. Eric gives the signal. Lights out. Spots on. Showtime.

After some bowing and waving at the end of the successful performance, the children join their parents in the school canteen for the after-show drink. Eric welcomes all the parents as they enter and he later stops at each table for a brief chat.

At the table where Emma and her husband are standing, the conversation turns by chance to cycling. Her husband boasts about the number of kilometres he cycles each week and how for him this is the best way to forget his daily worries and recharge his batteries. Eric listens to all this and wonders whether or not cycling might be the ideal way to get rid of those extra kilos. But the idea of spending all his free time flogging his guts out on a bike doesn't really appeal to him. However, when Emma butts in to say that her new electric bicycle gives her all the exercise she needs, Eric's ears prick up again. He listens as Emma explains how she began, why she opted for an electric bike and, above all, why she decided to buy a brand-X bike. She goes on to describe how the company contacted her a month later to ask if she had any ideas about how the brand-X cycling experience could be improved. What's more, when she passed the 1,000-kilometre mark on the company's app, they even sent her a free rain jacket to congratulate her! By now, Eric is 100 percent convinced. That evening, he orders the same brand-X bike online.

Everyone has various circles of personal contact and influence. In the short story above, you can see how Emma and Eric come into contact with several different groups each week. From the music school (which they are both involved in) to Emma's dog club and Eric's Whatsapp group for foodies.

As companies, we often limit ourselves to looking at our own sphere of influence, but it would be foolish to ignore the influence that that our team members and customers can have on our behalf. The above story illustrates the kind of conversation that takes place millions of times each day. Moreover, advertising campaigns and promotional stunts, no matter how smart, are simply not capable of generating these conversations, because they fall outside your company's direct sphere of influence. If you are brand-X, there is no easy way for you to approach a potential customer like Eric, above all because he didn't really know whether he wanted a bike or not. Thanks to Emma, brand-X now has a highly motivated new bike owner without having to spend a penny on expensive advertising and marketing. By taking a number of simple, cheap and automatic steps (user's app, free rain jacket, etc.), brand-X was able to convert Emma into a proud ambassador for their bikes. As a result, she now brings in new customers in her own unique way. Can you imagine the impact it would have if you were able to convert all your customers into an ambassador? Your company would grow exponentially.

COVEY'S CIRCLES OF INFLUENCE

In the diagram below, your company is in the centre of the circle. You are the stone that has been thrown into a pond or the hard core at the centre of a snowball. The more ambassadors you have, the wider the circles of influence around you will ripple out and the greater the impact you will have on them. Every time someone praises you or your products, your reach gets a tiny bit bigger. And the more people you get to know in this manner, the more they will spread your story still further.

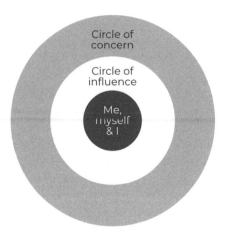

Steven R. Covey was an American author, businessman and keynote speaker. In 1996, he was listed by *Time Magazine* as one of the twenty-five most influential people on earth. In addition to publishing successful books, he was also a professor at the Huntsman School of Business and the University of Utah. In his universally praised book *The Seven Habits of Highly Effective People*, Covey divided the environment around us into two concentric circles: the circle of influence and the circle of concern.

If you want to have influence, the most important thing you need to assess is whether or not and how you can have impact on a situation. The key to success resides in understanding that you will achieve more if you know which people you can influence directly. In this respect, Covey argues that it is possible for you to act proactively to increase your influence. This generates a self-supporting process: you reach/achieve more, therefore you become more positive, therefore you reach/achieve even more.

When we talk about influence, we are actually talking about situations or people over which/whom we have influence (or not). In this context, it also important to know clearly how you can best deal with your influence. What are its limits? How can it be applied? Recognising the existence of both circles will give you greater insight into your own actions and help you to decide what is possible in any given circumstances. Covey regards these circles as a way to initiate a process of thought, to solve problems, and to map out situations.

The circles can also be used to show how it is possible to generate significant reactions through small actions and how you can stimulate people in your immediate environment to enthuse others in turn.

The circle of influence is the innermost circle and represents the situations and people over which/whom you have a degree of influence. Within this circle, your influence on these situations and people can either be direct or indirect. The most important aspect of this influence is that you can use it immediately and can use it without anyone's help. Verbs such as 'do', 'want', 'can', 'choose', etc. allow you to make clear exactly what you expect. These are also words that you can use as a facilitator. From an ambassadorship perspective, the main challenge (and the biggest potential reward) is situated in the sphere of influence of your team members. This is the circle in which family, friends, colleagues, fellow (sport) club enthusiasts, etc. are all located.

The family circle

In most cases, this is the closest and most tightly-knit circle, the circle in which we grow up and live. The level of trust in the family circle is high and its members often help each other. For example, a father might help his daughter to choose her first car or a grandson might advise his grandmother about the best smartphone to buy. The family circle is also the circle in which we spend most time. As a result, we attach greater value to opinions that are shared within that circle. And because so many things are discussed openly within the circle, we hear lots and lots of different recommendations and referrals. Where was that great restaurant? What is the best insurance policy to take out? When is the best time of year to book my holiday in Ibiza? Family members help each other to make better choices every day, by sharing their own experiences. The family circle starts with your immediate family (mother, father, brothers, sisters), but then spreads further to include your other relatives. Depending on the nature of the mutual relationships, second and third degree relatives can also exercise considerable influence.

Characteristics of the family circle: small, closely-knit, a high degree of trust, high impact, multiple contact moments.

The work circle

A large part of our life is also spent in our work circle. An average active person has roughly 112 'waking' hours at his/her disposal each week (assuming they sleep for an average number of hours). Of those 112 hours, work occupies between 40 and 45 hours on average. Over the course of a lifetime, this means a total of some 90,000 hours at our place of work. In other words, the work circle plays a major role in our life and helps to determine our sphere of influence to a significant degree.

The work circle not only contains our colleagues, but also customers, suppliers, visitors and even the employees of other companies working in the same location. These are all people who we meet physically or in online meetings, with whom we have lunch or discuss the latest Netflix series at the coffee machine. It is the desk clerk who wishes everyone a friendly good morning and lets you know when your latest Zalando package has been delivered. It is the cleaning team that tidies up your office each evening and arranges your paperwork neatly on your desk. Viewed in these terms, the work circle is a large group of people with whom we have formal and informal conversations on a daily basis. After your family, they are the people with whom you spend the most time.

Characteristics of the work circle: (very) extensive, professional in nature, moderate impact, diverse.

The friendship circle

If you are lucky, in addition to your family and your work you will have a number of friends, who will also play an important role in your life. Friends come in all shapes and sizes: you have close friends who you see regularly, but you also have friends from your youth, who you only see once a year at the annual school reunion. Much has been written about friendship and the various relationships between people, but there is no need for us to explore that here.

Suffice to say that people often seek the advice of their friends, if they need to make difficult choices. Our friends also influence our interests, sometimes even the clothes we wear. The term 'circle of friends' is an apt one. With young people, this circle sometimes closes tightly around its members to form an exclusive peer group: a coterie of like-minded people of similar age, status and interests, sometimes with a shared behavioural code. With adults, the circle of friends is generally more open, which theoretically makes it an ideal breeding ground for ambassadorship. On the downside, a circle of friends can frequently be large and wide-ranging, with no clearly defined boundaries. The line between a circle of friends and a circle of acquaintances is a thin one. Depending on a person's attitude towards relationships, it is possible to have either a very diverse or a very intimate circle of friends.

The circle of friends can have an influence on all age groups and all population groups, at all times and in all places. However, it is not always easy to determine how far ambassadorship is likely to reach.

Characteristics of the circle of friends: (very) large; varied in terms of impact; high level of trust among close friends, which diminishes with acquaintances.

The leisure circle

In their leisure time, people practise many different kinds of hobbies (sometimes more than one). The range of such hobbies is huge and incredibly varied. Some like to play football each weekend with the local pub team; others prefer to follow Italian cooking lessons on a Tuesday evening. You often practise your hobbies with other people, as a result of which new and relatively tight circles are formed. Within these circles, opinions are shared. In the football changing room the players might discuss which barbecue to buy. In the Italian kitchen health-conscious cooks might talk about the best kind of running shoes for people planning a marathon.

People who come together as a result of their similar interests automatically develop a bond and a form of trust. This bond goes beyond the narrow confines of their common hobby, so that opinions are valued on matters that have no connection with the hobby itself. This means, for example, that a seller of running shoes may find that he has acquired a group of new buyers because someone in an Italian cooking lesson has recommended his product. Or that the local barbecue store suddenly finds itself with an unexpected number of footballers among its most recent customers...

Characteristics of the leisure circle: limited, regular contact, large impact in clearly defined areas.

The community circle

Within society, we all belong to a number of different communities. For you, your town or city might form such a community. So, too, might the school where your children receive their education. Or perhaps it is the religious group to which you belong. The word 'community' implies that these are groupings in which people have 'something' in common: a neighbourhood, a language, concern for the environment, etc. These communities can also form circles in which people can recommend your products, services or whatever else you are selling.

Perhaps your company has been searching for a long time to recruit the right member of staff for a particular job. Occasionally, you chat with John at the school gate, while you are both waiting for the kids. He is a pleasant man, and clearly intelligent. During your conversations, you also learn that John is looking for a new job, one in which he can rediscover his passion. You recommend your company to John and you recommend John to your company. A match made in heaven, which would never have happened without your ambassadorship!

Characteristics of the community circle: very large, low impact, varied contacts.

In the course of our life, we all belong to a number of different circles. These circles are not all constant or unchanging, so that we can easily migrate from one circle to another. As a result, a person's spheres of influence are not something static; on the contrary, they tend to be fluid. They often form and reform organically and can evolve with considerable speed. This means that the level of impact created by converting someone into an ambassador is difficult to predict in advance. One ambassador might generate a dozen new customers during his first month, while a different ambassador might need to wait for three years before he can give the push that finally leads to the new megadeal you have all been waiting for. Ambassadors follow many different roads leading in many different directions, so that you are never quite certain where they are going to arrive or when. All you can be certain of is this: the more ambassadors you are able to mobilise, the greater your chances of success.

The community circle is one of the circles that is more distant from the centre in the Covey model. It is in the zone that Covey referred to as the circle of concern. This is the circle of things about which you are concerned or in which you are involved. As a result, they are also things through which you can be influenced directly or indirectly. On the reverse side of the coin, you are only able to exercise little or no influence on others. The verbs that you hear in these contexts tend to be 'have', 'wish', 'must', etc. To generate the positive movement you desire, you need to motivate others and secure their help to spread your message. In the circle of concern, you have to do everything you can to get your problem noticed and (hopefully) resolved. Do not assume too quickly that this will not be possible. Just give it a try! No matter how unlikely it might seem, there will always be people in the circle of concern who will be willing to communicate your message and spread it further, providing you give them the right encouragement and support. The possibilities will differ depending on the nature of the challenge or situation, but there will always be options you can pursue.

Beyond the circles of influence and concern, there is a vast area where you can do nothing at all on your own. Even so, by stimulating people to action in your two inner circles, you will still be able to create positive movement in the outer zone.

Remember that the fastest results are always achieved from within the circle of influence, since this is the place where you can exert your influence directly.

Proactive people always focus on the circle of influence. They do not put the blame for their own limitations on others, but instead use positive energy to try and enlarge their circle of influence by being constantly active with its boosting and improvement.

In this respect, a good team can have a huge impact on an organisation. In your organisation, you too as an individual will unquestionably also have impact, but in this example it is clear that this impact is in the third circle. The team has wide-ranging influence, but your personal influence is smaller.

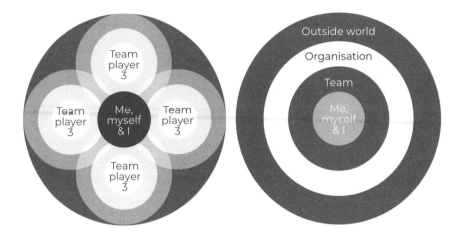

SIX DEGREES OF KEVIN BACON

Another model that perfectly illustrates the limitless possibilities and reach of ambassadorship is Six Degrees of Kevin Bacon. It is a popular parlour game where the aim is to link Hollywood personalities through their film roles to star actor Kevin Bacon in a maximum of six steps. For example, Pam Grier can be linked to Kevin Bacon in three steps, because she acted in *Escape from L.A.* with Peter Fonda, who in turn played in *Easy Rider* with Jack Nicholson, who in turn was Kevin Bacon's courtroom opponent in *A Few Good Men*. Six Degrees of Kevin Bacon can be played with many different categories and is based on the theory of the six degrees of separation, which was first formulated following the so-called 'small world' experiment.

This experiment was carried out in the 1960s by the psychologist Stanley Milgram to investigate just how closely people were connected to each other. Milgram sent letters to 160 people in the state of Nebraska, gave them the name and address of a stockbroker in Boston, and instructed them to send on the letter to another friend or acquaintance who might be able to help move the letter closer to the stockbroker. Each person who received the chain letter was asked to do the same, until it eventually arrived at someone who knew the stockbroker personally, at which point the letter could be sent to him directly.

By the end of the experiment, Milgram was able to conclude that most of the letters reached the stockbroker after just five or six steps. On the basis of these findings a theory was developed that everyone in the world was connected to everyone else by six degrees of separation. This, of course, then became the origin of the Six Degrees of Kevin Bacon game.

Milgram also discovered that half of the letters reached the stockbroker with just three intermediary steps. In other words, although everyone is separated from each other by no more than six stages, there is a smaller group of people who are connected to a disproportionately large number of others, with only a few degrees of separation between them. The members of this small group are generally known as the connectors. The idea that a handful of people can spread your message better than the rest of the population is now known as the social influence theory and it has been a standard element in marketing philosophy for more than 50 years. Connectors usually have links to a number of different communities: because of their job, their hobbies, their beliefs, their experiences, etc. Their power lies in their involvement with many different worlds, which they are able to bring together in a way that would otherwise not be possible. If you can convert these connectors into your ambassadors, your message will spread much further and much faster, so that your approval and recognition ratings will shoot through the roof.

DIGITAL VS. LIVE

The backbone of ambassador marketing is real conversations between real people. Authentic interactions are the foundation of any effective ambassador strategy. There are hundreds of techniques for boosting digital recommendations, but these often involve interactions that are impersonal. This explains why they are so frequently perceived as being a cheap marketing trick. If you want to send true ambassadors out into the world to promote your company, make sure that they are willing and able to talk about you in real and genuine day-to-day conversations.

Nowadays, our lives are dominated by screens. Each morning when we wake up, the first thing we do, often while still in bed, is to check the news or our missed messages on our smartphone. Once down in the kitchen, we read our digital newspaper on our tablet over breakfast (unless it is Saturday, in which case many people still get a real newspaper, made of... paper). We then work several hours a day on our laptop or computer, although between our different zoom meetings and work sessions we still pull out our smartphones to check that we have not missed anything important. Even during the coffee break and at lunch, we exchange online films and funnies to amuse our colleagues. When we finally get home in the evening, we flop down in front of our smart-TV to binge-watch the latest Netflix series, before ending our fun-filled day with a quick scroll on Instagram or TikTok.

The 2021 Digimeter, which investigates and maps out media use in Flanders, revealed how the corona crisis immersed many people in a high-speed digital bath. No fewer than 11 percent of the people questioned acquired an additional digital screen during the lockdown and more than half had access to at least one paid streaming service. In comparison with previous years, the average screen time per day has increased by more than 30 minutes and now stands at a total of 185 minutes, or just over three hours.[4]

Of course, not everyone's day looks like that, at least not every day. Even so, it gives a realistic impression of how many people now experience much of their life through the medium of a screen. It is not our intention here to argue in favour of less screen time. That would be like trying to turn back the tide. However, the above figures make clear that at the present time the lives of the majority of people in the western world are experienced digitally or even virtually. Like it or not, screens have become mainstream – and they are here to stay. Screens are now so massively present in day-to-day life that the largest part of most companies' media budget will be devoted to them. From television commercials to Facebook adverts, the virtual and digital channels dominate the advertising world. Virtual ad boards and messages have become the new norm, while real-world communication is steadily declining.

During the past three years, the gross level of media spending has fallen.[5] In 2018, this fall amounted to 1.5%. In 2019, it was 1.9%. In 2020, the first corona year, the cutback in gross media investment was equivalent to 10.7% (offline media -14.7%) in comparison with the 2019 figure. This means that total media investment has now fallen back to the 2013 level. The largest decrease was noted in cinema advertising (-64.9%), followed by home-delivered advertising folders (-57.3%), outdoor (billboard) advertising (-23.3%), magazines (-18%), newspapers (-15.6%), radio (-14.4%) and TV (-10.1%).

Online advertising was the only medium that recorded an increase (+17.5%) during this extraordinary year.

At the same time, a recent study by RTL/AdConnect has shown that screen consumption in the western world has increased dramatically. The amount of time we spend in front of screens has risen almost everywhere and now amounts to a daily average of some 220 minutes, or more than four and a half hours!

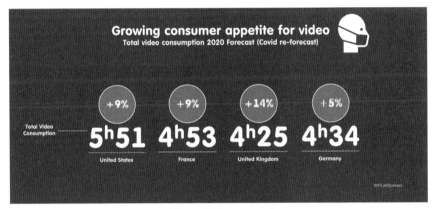

© RTL AdConnect Video consumption 2020

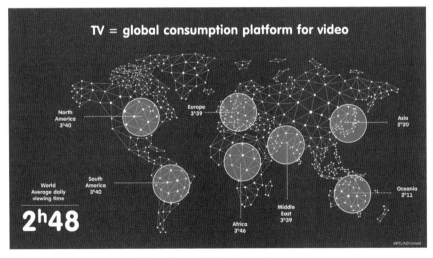

© RTL AdConnect Video consumption 2020

The effect of these evolutions means that advertising on screens is becoming more expensive, while its impact is decreasing. Thanks to the use of advanced techniques, such as retargeting or AI-guided advertising, digital advertising in general is still becoming ever more efficient, but this is more than necessary, because consumers are becoming less sensitive to its appeal. Do you remember the first time you saw an automatically generated advert after you had visited a particular website? Amazing! Magic! Nowadays, this practice has become so standard that we are almost immune to it. In some cases, digitalisation has been taken so far that many companies, particularly tech companies, only continue to exist in the digital world. They have no physical premises, no own product and no recognisable presence in physical reality. As a result, they are urgently looking for new ways to break into the daily lives of their users.

This trend offers some interesting opportunities. In the real world, communication and marketing are gaining ground. The real experience of real products has become the perfect way to cut through the monotonous daily routine of our screen-based existence. The success of Sunday in creating textile collections for brands is confirmation of the value of physical, tangible products. Merchandising helps brands to enter the physical world of the consumer and, as it were, tear their attention away from their screens. Time after time, companies have been hugely impressed once they see how their brand can be translated into (or onto) physical products. Similarly, the recipients of these products are delighted when they can finally get a t-shirt or a pair of socks of the brands of which they are such huge fans.

One obvious reason why physical experience and tangible products are such a powerful tool for brand expression is the fact that people, unlike many of the brands themselves and notwithstanding their own increasing screen consumption, continue to live in the real world. People can certainly have an online presence, with a profile and an e-mail address, but this is just a flat and one-dimensional version of reality. A personal conversation has much greater impact than any text message, e-mail or even video call can ever have. The COVID-19 pandemic and its resulting lockdowns have emphasised worldwide the importance of physical contact between people. Life is live! By nature, we human beings are social creatures who thrive on personal connection. Do you want to make a massive impact with your company or brand? If so, you need to find a way to convert people into ambassadors, so that you can become the talking point of real conversations. In the following chapter, you will learn, step by step and circle by circle, how you can involve more and more people with your brand, ultimately turning them into true ambassadors.

ACTION POINTS

In this chapter, we have learnt that your relationship with your customers and your employees is not one-dimensional, but that in their role as an ambassador they are able to exercise influence on different circles of people at the same time. As a business leader, this offers you a huge range of possibilities to generate impact in many new areas and on many new potential leads.

The first exercise you need to complete is to map out your own circles. When you draw out these circles on paper, you will be amazed by the extent of your network. Start with your own immediate family, your relatives and your best friends. After this, add a new circle for each domain in which you are active. This can range from playing for your pub football team each weekend to your membership of the local chamber of commerce. Finish by adding outer circles for groups with which you are associated, but where the connection cannot be described as 'close'. Sometimes, circumstances will dictate to which circle you belong at a particular moment in time. For example, you might feel yourself to be a Londoner when talking to other Englishmen, an Englishman when talking to a Scot (or an Irishman or Welshman) and a Brit when talking to a European or American. Remember also that, just like you, everyone else has a similar set of circles of their own. This should make clear to you the importance of investing heavily in ambassadors, because their impact can be enormous.

Which of the circles you have drawn are important for your company? Which products or services do you provide that might be interesting for some of these circles? If you are selling bikes, you will be more interested in a circle that contains a cycling club than a tennis club. But think carefully about other possible connections. Even though you are a bike seller, it would be useful for you to have ambassadors in local schools and in the town hall. Try to be clear and accurate about which circles you can benefit from and vice versa. Make a note of these 'special' circles.

Now that you know which circles are most important for your company, you can actively focus on them. When you ask your customers for recommendations, ask them specifically for recommendations in the circles that are likely to work for you. Because that is what a good recommendation does: it works on your behalf. If we return to the example of our bike seller, it seems clear that he can probably benefit most from recommendations made by the members of the cycling club. For this reason, whenever he sells a bike to a member of the club he always sends his new customer the following message:

> 'Thank you for shopping at my store. As you know, I am a small and independent trader, which means that I do not have a huge marketing budget to promote my business. I need to rely primarily on word of mouth to sell my bikes. If you are satisfied with the service I have provided, could you please let that be known in the cycling club. I would be eternally grateful.'

Asking for recommendations in this way is highly targeted, but also highly effective. It is the 'live' version of the online 'like'. Word of mouth is an important (if not the most important) source of product information that plays a key role in influencing the purchasing decisions of consumers. Online forms of appreciation, such as those posted on Tripadvisor, have been shown to have an impact on people making bookings and purchases via the internet. A study by BrightLocal,[6] a London company that specialises in marketing tools, revealed that 89 percent of consumers take customer reviews into account when deciding whether or not a company is reliable. Some 73 percent of the respondents also said that a positive review would persuade them to trust a product. A further study by Weber Shandwick,[7] a highly respected PR agency, concluded that consumers in Belgium attach a higher level of importance to the opinions of family and friends than the European average.

It is also worth noting that there is a significant body of research to show that when something is recommended verbally and spontaneously, this is experienced as being more accurate and more genuinely meant than when the same recommendation is made in written form, in which case the author has had more time to formulate and order his thoughts.

Conclusion? Asking for the right recommendation at the right moment in the right way can pay massive dividends. Knowing in which circle your best potential customers are located is a unique trump card in your ambassador marketing strategy.

'A person who feels appreciated will always do more than expected.'

Amy Rees Anderson

You can quickly and easily strengthen the impact that your current ambassadors are already having by simply thanking them and showing your appreciation for them in a sincere manner. Using the following three action points, you can already make a start, without the need to incur huge costs but in a way that will nonetheless have a huge impact on both you and your company. As an added bonus, it will allow you to make lots of different people very, very happy.

1   Telephone the customers who have given you a positive reference.

Put in a call to all the satisfied customers who have ever given you a reference (it doesn't matter how long ago) and thank them profusely for their positive recommendation. By telling them clearly and sincerely what their reference has meant for your company, you will let them see that what they have done and you have achieved is by no means self-evident. On the contrary, it is something out of the ordinary. In this way, they will know that you have carefully monitored the results of their recommendation and that you will continue to do so in the future. Take enough time to complete this important task properly.

2   Thank your enthusiastic team members publically.

Thank all your team members who consistently and unfailingly represent your company as true ambassadors, spreading your message far and wide, day after day. Far too often, this is (incorrectly) regarded as 'part of the job', but it is so much more than that. Be aware that the larger your organisation becomes, the harder it will be to find such 'super-spreaders'. By thanking them publically in the presence of other team members, so that they know beyond doubt that you appreciate what they do, you will help to prevent such valuable employees from being forgotten or, even worse, leaving the company.

3   Thank your early fans for their support

Who has believed in you throughout your career, right from the very first day your company was founded? Your partner? Your children and your parents? Probably (at least we hope so!), and probably before they even had anything that they could meaningfully spread as ambassadors. Thank them sincerely for always being there for you and/or your company and for continuing to believe in you and your project.

This might all sound a bit soppy and sentimental, but never underestimate the power of appreciation. The impact that you will notice once you have done these three things will amaze you. It not only strengthens your bond with your existing ambassadors, but stimulates them to recommend you even more strongly than in the past. Which in turn will lead to greater name recognition and an increased number of customers.

CHAPTER 3

THE SCIENCE OF RECOMMENDATIONS

WHY AMBASSADORS ARE THE BEST YARDSTICK TO MEASURE GROWTH

In December 2003, Frederick F. Reichheld, a retired director of Bain & Company, published the results of a revolutionary study in the *Harvard Business Review*. He had set himself the ambitious task of discovering the ultimate question that a company can ask its customers, so that the growth of the company can be accurately predicted. In other words, he attempted to define a single question, the answer to which would serve as an objective indicator for the company's future growth, a single score that would predict future success (or failure) and would work in every sector. Until this time, specialised (read 'expensive') companies had been hired to perform this task, using long, boring and often inaccurate questionnaires to establish the feelings and opinions of customers.

Reichheld decided to achieve his goal by organising a large-scale research project, limiting the number of questions to a maximum of twenty. He then sent the resultant questionnaire to more than four thousand of his former customers, active in many different sectors, requesting that they indicate which of the twenty questions best matched the results and position of their own company. Here are some examples of his questions:

- How strongly do you agree that [company X] is worthy of your loyalty?
- How strongly do you agree that [company X] sets the standard for excellence in your branch?
- How satisfied are you with the general performance of [company X]?

The results of the questionnaire were carefully analysed to see which question and answer corresponded most closely with fast or slow growth. For example, Reichheld investigated whether there was a connection between the number of people giving a 10 score to the question 'How satisfied are you with the general performance of [company X]?' and the fact that the company in question then grew faster than its competitors in the same branch.

After more than twelve months of analysing the questionnaires, Reichheld and his team had gathered enough information to publish fourteen conclusive case studies. The results were remarkable – and crystal clear. In eleven of the fourteen studies, the question 'How probable is it that you will recommend [company X] to a friend or colleague' was first or second in the ranking. In other words, in the large majority of cases this question had the closest correlation with the actual growth of the test companies. Companies that scored high for the question were also the companies that exhibited the strongest growth in their branch.

This study demonstrated in black and white that the ambassadorship of your customers is the most important driver for growth. True, it does not always guarantee growth, but without it you can never hope to achieve healthy and profitable growth.

Fascinated by the results of his own research, Reichheld decided to dig even deeper. He now wanted to know why ambassadorship is such a good indicator of future growth. Eventually, he concluded that recommendations are the strongest and most reliable yardstick for loyalty and growth because of the amount of effort that customers actually need to make to positively recommend your company. Ambassadors for your product or service do far more than simply indicating to others that opting for the said product or service is an economically responsible decision. By making this recommendation, they are also consciously putting their own reputation on the line. And people will only put their reputation at risk if they are convinced by and loyal to the company or brand in question.

Companies invest large amounts of time and money in complex tools that are designed to assess and quantify customer satisfaction. But all too often they are measuring the wrong things. The best predictor of turnover growth can usually be summarised in the following single question: Would you recommend this company to a friend?

Loyalty has a clear impact on the profitability of a company. Although loyal customers are not always profitable per se, the fact that they choose to remain faithful to your product or service generally reduces your company's acquisition costs. Loyalty also stimulates higher turnover. It is self-evident that no company can ever hope to grow if its outflow of customers is greater than its inflow. Loyalty helps to stem at least part of the outflow. Moreover, customers who are truly loyal have a tendency as time passes to buy more and more, spending a large portion of their income on a company that makes them feel good.

The results of Reichheld's study were later used to formulate the concept of the Net Promoter Score (or NPS), which expresses the number of a company's promoters or ambassadors in relation to the number of neutral or negative customers. A company that wants to grow must have more promoters than detractors. The only path that leads to profitable and sustainable growth is the path that will allow you to convert your loyal customers into true ambassadors.

THE RETURN OF AN AMBASSADOR: ALI & ALI

When Niels and his partner, Zymcke, bought a house a couple of years ago, they knew that the roof was no longer in good condition. There was asbestos panelling under the tiles, the chimney was crooked and the guttering was half hanging off. It was time to renew the roof completely – and the sooner, the better! They were convinced it would never survive another winter. Logically enough, they approached a number of different roofing companies for an estimate of the work involved and the likely cost.

A few weeks passed and nothing happened. Eventually, one or two of the contractors turned up to give the roof a cursory once-over, but disappeared from the scene almost as quickly as they had arrived. Perhaps now, at long last, an estimate would be forthcoming? Not a bit of it! It was another three weeks before a letter finally dropped onto their doormat, but the hopes of Niels and his partner were soon dashed. The contractor was more than happy to do the work and his price seemed not unreasonable, but it would be at least another year before he could start!

This was clearly not an option. Discouraged and almost at his wit's end, Niels decided as a last resort to post his request for an estimate on a portal website that served all the local contractors in the region. Within a quarter of an hour he received a telephone call from Ali. Ali explained that he and his partner (also named Ali) ran their own company that in normal circumstances specialised in work for the government and local authorities. However, the corona crisis and the resulting suspension of public sector contracts meant that they had been forced to turn their attention to the private sector as the only way to keep their workers fully employed. For this reason, Ali asked if it would be okay if he came and had a look at the roof the next day. Niels was over the moon! He had been getting nowhere for the best part of two months, but now it looked as though he would be helped in less than 24 hours! Well done, Ali! At last, someone who knew how to communicate quickly and clearly.

As promised, Ali & Ali arrived promptly at the agreed time the next day and gave the roof a thorough inspection. Their verdict was worse than expected. Not only was the roof devoid of insulation, but the beam structure was also on its last legs and urgently needed replacing. 'Prevention is better than cure' thought Niels and Zymcke, and so they decided to have everything done all in one go. Why risk having the roof cave in on them? They confirmed this to A&A, who promised to let them have a full estimate within seven days. Following its approval, they could start the work two weeks later. This was music to Niels' ears: they had found the solution they were looking for.

The work started on schedule and was carried out to perfection. If minor problems arose during the implementation, they were put right without any additional cost. Again, this was only possible because of the excellent communication with Ali & Ali. They were always contactable throughout the day via the channels that had been stipulated in advance. Anything that needed to be discussed, was discussed, agreed and arranged with a minimum of delay. Upon completion of each phase of the project, the contractors provided a detailed report, complete with photographs. This clear and open communication, combined with the excellence of the craftsmanship, not only put Niels and Zymcke at ease, but soon converted them into true Ali & Ali ambassadors. They recommended the company to everyone in their immediate family, with further projects as a result. First, the renovation of Niels' parental home; then the refurbishment of his mother's shop; and finally a new bathroom in his parents-in-law's house. All courtesy of Ali & Ali!

Because they had completed the first project to such a high standard and had exceeded Niels and Zymcke's expectations, they were able to turn two satisfied customers into two ardent ambassadors. As a result, they were able to attract a series of further projects without spending a single eurocent of their marketing budget. And it didn't end there: if anyone looking for a building contractor asks Niels for advice, there is still only one name he recommends: Ali & Ali.

THE CUSTOMER VALUE MATRIX

There are different ways to measure the value of your current crop of customers. How often do they order? How much do they order? Am I making too much money from some customers, so that I might frighten them off? Am I making too little money from some customers, so that there is room to increase my margin?

A clear and powerful model to estimate the value of your customers is the Customer Value Matrix, first developed by Kumar, Petersen and Leone. They investigated different ways in which the value of customers can be assessed and, in particular, sought to find ways that would allow the most profitable customers to be identified.

The essence of their theory is that it is not only important take into account of how much a customer orders, but also how often he recommends your company, product or service to others. These two figures are added to a 2x2 matrix, which results in the classification of customers into one of four categories.

The two crucial figures in this concept are therefore the following:

1   The Customer Lifetime Value (CLV) of a customer is the value that indicates how much that customer will spend in your company in relation to an average customer. Or to put it another way: the CLV is the estimated turnover of a customer during his full business lifetime. The higher the CLV, the better the customer he is.

2   The Customer Referral Value (CRV) is the turnover that customers generate directly or indirectly through their recommendations of your company. A high CRV means that the customer concerned is a loyal ambassador who will often attract new customers for you, even if they are often smaller ones.

In other words, the Customer Value Matrix not only takes into account the personal turnover of the customer, but also the turnover he generates in others. The mapping and comparison of the CLV and CRV make it possible to distinguish four different types of customer.

Misers

These are the customers who are least beneficial to your company. They have a low CLV and therefore spend relatively little money on your products and/or services. In addition, they also have a low CRV, so that they provide you with hardly any new or potential customers. Customers of the miser type will not help your company to grow. On the contrary, your turnover will stagnate and your customer portfolio will remain, static at best.

Affluents

There are your best customers in terms of what they spend on your products and/or services. Yet even though they are loyal to your company, they seldom (if ever) recommend it to others. In other words, their CLV is high and their CRV is low. Customers of the affluent type are highly beneficial for your current business situation, but will not provide you with an inflow of new customers in the future.

Advocates

Advocates are customers who frequently and successfully recommend your company to others. They tend not to be major customers, but they are passionate about what you do and will provide you with a steady stream of new customers in the future. Advocates are often the most underrated type of customer and therefore often overlooked. Their lack of real purchasing power means that their CLV is relatively low and their CRV-boosting activities seldom make the limelight. Even so, thanks to their recommendatory behaviour they have a significant impact on your future turnover.

Champions

These customers must be your absolute top priority. They spend lots of money on your products and/or services and bring in lots of new customers as well. This combination of a high CLV and a high CRV is a marriage made in business heaven! Every ambitious company that wishes to move forward must do everything in its power to turn as many of its customers as possible into this kind of champion. In that respect, reading this book and focusing your attention in the future on ambassador marketing is a big step in the right direction!

Once you are familiar with the distribution of these four segments in your company, it is easier to develop more specific marketing campaigns, because it is clearer in which direction you want your various customers to evolve.

As far as the champions are concerned, all you need to do is to keep them happy. So make sure that you give them no reason not to be happy. Continue to communicate with them in an open manner and give them a little extra treat every once in a while. You don't really need to make any extra marketing effort with this group to keep them on board. If your products/services remain at the same level or even improve, this will happen automatically.

Your affluents are the customers you would really like to promote into champions. They are good customers who spend a lot and spend it frequently, but you need to stimulate them to talk about your company more. Much more. You can do this by inviting them to special events or by providing them with merchandising items. This will give them a good reason to talk about your company with others. You can also use marketing techniques that stimulate 'word of mouth' advertising, such as member-gets-member campaigns. Alternatively, you can write customer stories about them, which they can then share and which will give others a reason to approach them, a conversation in which you will inevitably be a part.

As for your advocates, you need to encourage them to spend more on your products and services. They are already your proud ambassadors and talk about your company all the time, so there is no need to make further effort in this direction. Think about the possibilities of cross-selling or promotions that will allow them to become more familiar with your range of products and/or services. This will bring you a double return: not only an increase in turnover as a result of greater direct sales to the customers in question, but also yet more new customers, as they sing the praises of an even greater range of your goods. For this reason, this is the group that offers you the greatest potential for progress in the future.

'Just having satisfied customers isn't good enough anymore. If you really want a booming business, you have to create raving fans.'

Ken Blanchard (co-author of The One Minute Manager)

Your misers pose the hardest challenge. You need to stimulate them in both directions: more sales and more recommendations. Launch marketing campaigns designed to increase their Customer Lifetime Value, but also try to boost their Customer Referral Value by methods similar to those you use on the affluents. Your aim in the first instance is to turn your misers into affluents as well. But who knows: if your campaigns are good enough, you might even be able to convert them into champions!

Try to gear all your marketing efforts to matching the needs and profiles of these four very different categories. There is no point in sending marketing communications designed to push greater sales to customers who are already spending at the limit of their financial capacity. Similarly, offering bonuses for extra recommendations to customers who are already pushing your company as often as they can is not money well spent. In fact, it might even be counterproductive, since these superfans might not understand why they are thought to be in need of this additional 'stimulation'. So think carefully about what kind of marketing messages you send and who you send them to. This will not only reduce your marketing costs, but also increase the effectiveness and return of your marketing actions.

In short, a 'one size fits all' approach is not possible if you want to take proper account of the segmentation in the Customer Value Matrix. You need to develop a separate marketing and communication strategy for each of the four profiles that most closely matches their particular sensitivities. This is the only way to increase your chances of success.

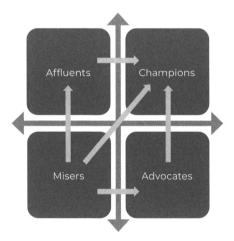

Customer Lifetime Value – V. Kumar is professor of marketing and executive director of the Center for Excellence in Brand & Customer Management at the University of Georgia – J. Mack Robinson College of Business.

By making sure that you do not send messages to customers who neither want nor need them, you will save a significant part of your marketing budget that you can then spend in other areas and other segments, where that money will have a much greater impact.

TESLA'S FOUNDERS SERIES

Tesla can count on a group of very loyal customers. As a new Tesla costs the best part of 70,000 euros, the members of this group nearly all belong to the affluent category. Elon Musk is very familiar with the Customer Value Matrix and well aware of the power of ambassadorship.

In 2018, Musk and his team developed a brilliant marketing campaign to try and convert more of these affluents into ambassadorial champions. They launched an action whereby the existing owners of Model S Teslas would receive a 1,000 euro credit if they could bring in a new Tesla customer. This new customer also received an immediate 1,000 euro discount on his new car. At first glance, 1,000 euros might seem like a lot of money, but if you work it out it only amounts to an average discount of around one percent.

To lend the campaign extra power, Tesla also dangled two other carrots in front of its existing owners. Anyone who brought in five new buyers was offered a private tour around the Tesla Giga factory with a guest of their choice. But if you brought in ten new customers, you were given access to the new and super-exclusive 'Founders Series' of the Model X, a model personally inspected by Elon Musk himself.

Tesla is a past master at converting affluents into champions. They understand perfectly that although Customer Lifetime Value is important, in the long term Customer Referral Value is perhaps even more crucial for the future of the company.

AMBASSADOR MARKETING VS. TRADITIONAL ADVERTISING

Imagine that you have been given a marketing budget of 100 euros to spend. Obviously, you will want to spend that money wisely and preferably in the channels that will bring you the biggest return.

Numerous studies have shown that a recommendation from a friend or a family member has the greatest impact on people's purchasing decisions.

EXPONENTIAL GROWTH IN AMBASSADORS, THANKS TO THE BANDWAGON EFFECT

To understand the bandwagon effect, we need to go back to the presidential elections in 19th century America. During the 1848 election, an entertainer named Dan Rice travelled around the country in a wagon, on which a small band was playing. The aim was to drum up support for the candidacy of Zachary Taylor. The wagon would ride into town, the band would start playing, and Rice encouraged local people to jump onto the back of the wagon and start dancing. This attracted other people, so that there was soon a large crowd. Not all of these people were supporters of Taylor. Even so, they were still 'exposed' to his political message. The idea soon caught on and Taylor won the election by a landslide. By the end of the 19th century, bandwagons had become a prominent part of nearly every political campaign. Of course, actual bandwagons no longer exist, but the term 'jump on the bandwagon' has survived and is used to describe the social phenomenon of wanting to belong to the majority, even if that goes against your convictions!

In other words, the bandwagon effect is a psychological phenomenon, as a result of which a certain opinion becomes increasingly believed in relation to the growing number of people who support it. Put simply, the more active superfans an opinion (or product or service) has, the greater the likelihood that even more people will be persuaded to become a fan. This phenomenon is so powerful that in certain circumstances it can even override the economic theory of supply and demand. Supply and demand is based on the premise that consumers make their decisions based exclusively on price and their own personal preferences. However, scientific research has now shown the people's purchasing decisions can also be strongly influenced by others. As a result, some of the most fundamental economic models (supply and demand is just one of them) have been turned upside down, or are at least now the subject of discussion.

Studies suggest that today's consumers are spending less and less time on the collection of objective and reliable information about the goods and services they are planning to buy and are relying increasingly on the opinions and purchasing behaviour of others. We are probably all familiar with the phenomenon of choosing a restaurant where people are already sitting, since this (or so we think) is indirect evidence of the quality of the restaurant. A full restaurant must be good; an empty restaurant must be bad.

At the start of the 1980s, this was something that the owners of the Pacha chain of discotheques exploited brilliantly. They hired in groups of young people (mostly attractive women) to dance in their clubs as soon as the doors opened, preferably in locations that were visible from the street. The idea was to tempt passers-by to come in and join them – and it worked! This was just one of the many smart marketing strategies used by Pacha, but it helps to explain why their franchise-brand is now known all around the world.

Nowadays, the bandwagon effect can perhaps be most clearly seen in the hype on social media. In 2019, the Finnish food blogger Jenni Häyrinen launched a recipe for baked pasta with feta that went viral on TikTok and Instagram, so that in no time at all many supermarkets had sold their entire stock of the famous Greek cheese. The American supermarket chain The Fresh Market reported a 45 percent increase in the sale of feta as a result of this one recipe.

Another (and very visual) example of the bandwagon effect is the long rows of waiting customers that you often see outside Apple stores whenever a new iPhone is launched. The more people standing in the queue, the greater the sense of urgency becomes amongst other members of the public to buy the phone before supplies run out. As a result, they also join the queue and sales skyrocket!

Ambassador marketing makes use of the psychological power of this bandwagon effect to the benefit of your brand. Because more and more people are stimulated to talk about you, other people will also want to learn more about your company, as a result of which they will start talking about you as well. This ultimately leads to steady and sustainable growth, as your ambassadors continue to bring in further waves of new customers.

AMBASSADOR MARKETING METRICS

'Without data you're just another person with an opinion.'

W. Edwards Deming

There are various figures or metrics that you can monitor to measure the ROI of your ambassador marketing programme. The old business adage says that 'measuring is knowing', so that when you invest in the development of your ambassador network you need to be sure that your investment is actually having the desired effect. The data that merits your attention can be divided into three broad categories: participation, activity and conversion. By measuring these three categories, you will get a clear picture of the success or otherwise of your ambassador marketing programme, so that it can be corrected or further improved, where necessary.

Participation metrics

Number of ambassadors

Like all marketing channels, researching the data for your ambassador channel is crucial if you wish to generate a greater return (which, after all, is the name of the game). The 'participation' category covers all facts and figures that relate to your ambassadors, the most important of which is their total number. Even though this is a relatively easy figure to determine, it is still important to keep a regular check on its movement.

How many people do you recognise and accept as being ambassadors of your company? To answer this question properly, you first need to define exactly what criteria an ambassador must meet. Depending on the size of your company and the sector in which you operate, you are free to choose who you regard as being an ambassador and who not.

Here are some suggestions for the types of people who you can certainly consider for inclusion in your ambassadorship programme:

- your closest stakeholders, such as your personnel, partners, family, etc.;
- people with whom you regularly interact on social media;
- people who have referred others to your company;
- people who place positive reviews about your company;
- (very) regular customers with whom you have a personal connection.

Nowadays, there are a number of software tools, such as HubSpot or Salesforce, which give you the option to label people as an evangelist/ambassador. This status is seen as being the ultimate step in the customer relationship. If you make use of a CRM system or some other customer database, you can allocate this same status to some of your customers. In this way, you can keep a check on how many ambassadors you have and how many new ones you acquire each month.

Example

Each month, ten people start to act as ambassadors for your company. This means that your group of ambassadors will grow by ten people twelve times in the course of a year. By the end of the first year, you should therefore have 120 ambassadors.

Number of ambassadors after one year = 120

Number of active ambassadors

The above example is just the first and very simple step in your monitoring of your ambassador marketing. However, remember to also take account of the fact that every person registered as an ambassador will remain an ambassador for the rest of his/her life. Removing him/her from the system is no longer possible. But will they continue to remain active on your behalf throughout this period? More advanced metrics systems also keep a check on the activity level of your ambassadors. How many recommendations do they make for your company and how often? You can link this level of (in) activity to certain criteria. For example, if someone fails to make a single recommendation in a 12-month period, you can use this as a criterion for no longer regarding him/her as an active ambassador.

Example

As in the previous example, you get ten new ambassadors each month, so that in numerical terms your group of ambassadors has grown to 120 by the end of the first year. However, you notice that 30 percent of these people are no longer making recommendations on your behalf, so that they can no longer be regarded as active ambassadors.

Number of active ambassadors after one year = 120 - 30% = 80

Reproduction number – virality

If you want to take things another step further, you can measure the reproduction number or virality of your ambassadors. During the corona epidemic, we have all become familiar with the experts talking about the reproduction number of the virus, but you can apply the same principle to your ambassadors, with your brand or company serving (metaphorically speaking!) as the virus. How many new ambassadors do your existing ambassadors bring in? If the reproduction number of your ambassador programme is more than R=1, you will benefit from viral growth. This will happen if, for example, every ambassador brings in two new customers, who in turn also become ambassadors, thereby creating a kind of snowball effect. Your ambassadors keep on doubling themselves exponentially, like a snowball rolling unstoppably down a mountainside.

Example

If an ambassador brings in two other new ambassadors, this results in a reproduction figure of R =2. In this case, the further growth in the number of your ambassadors will be exponential, as shown in the figures below. The higher the reproduction number, the faster the number of new ambassadors increases.

Growth in ambassadors when R = 2: 1–2–4–8–16–32–64–128–256–512

Activity metrics

Number of recommendations per ambassador

Of course, the number of active ambassadors is not the only metric you need to keep an eye on. The number of recommendations per ambassador is another excellent indicator for assessing the output of your ambassadors. Does every ambassador bring in an average of one new customer or ten new customers? It is obviously in your own best interests that your ambassadors work as efficiently and as effectively as possible, and in chapter 4 we will suggest a number of measures that will allow you to increase the return of your ambassadorial programme by 'training' your ambassadors to make more and better recommendations.

Do not confine your monitoring of activity to averages. You also need to check the spread. Are there ambassadors who are head and shoulders above the rest in terms of the number of recommendations they make? Is it clear why these ambassadors score better than everyone else? Can you spot particular trends to explain this, such as certain types of recommendations or certain periods of the year?

Example 69

You have ten ambassadors, who on average each make two recommendations per year. This is not bad, but you would like to have more. However, you have now been trying to increase this average figure for a couple of years, but so far without success. As a result, you decide to look more closely at the spread of the recommendations. This reveals that nine of your ambassadors only make a single recommendation each year, whereas the tenth ambassador makes a massive eleven recommendations! This still makes twenty recommendations in total, which accounts for the average figure of two per ambassador, but it also makes clear that if you want to boost this average you will need to find out how and why one super-ambassador is making more recommendations than all the other ambassadors put together! This will then help you to devise a strategy that will allow the majority to improve their level of activity.

Potential turnover per ambassador

Quantity and quality go hand in hand. You cannot measure one without measuring the other. If you only measure the number of your recommendations, you will be making a serious mistake, because the quality of these recommendations is just as important. You must measure this as well, because there can be huge differences. What is better: a recommendation leading to a sale of 50 euros or a recommendation leading to a sale of 50,000 euros? The answer is obvious.

A useful metric to monitor in this respect is the potential turnover that each ambassador can be expected to generate. Once again, you need to look at average potential turnover, but must also identify your top guns, because they will show you what is ultimately possible. Remember, however, that potential turnover is not the same as actual turnover. Many things can go wrong during the sales process, and this is more likely to be the fault of your own company and products than the fault of your ambassador.

For this reason, it is unwise to only measure confirmed sales, because this might mean that you are missing out on a huge untapped reserve of potential income. Keeping this metric is also crucial for your marketing plan, because it allows you to measure with precision how much potential turnover each of your ambassadors yields for your company and therefore how much you can reasonably spend on supporting your ambassador marketing programme.

Example

An ambassador makes an average of two recommendations per year with a potential turnover of 1,000 euros per recommendation. Once you have this data, you can take steps to improve it. How can you boost the potential turnover per recommendation? This might be possible, for example, through training or by offering a unique item that is only made available to ambassadors (and, by chance, happens to cost 1,500 euros).

Conversion metrics

Conversion percentage

The conversion percentage of your ambassadors is the number of deals they have secured, divided by the number of their recommendations. By measuring on average how many of your potential deals you were able to convert in practice, you can predict the return that your ambassadors are likely to provide in future. Remember, however, that the conversion percentage is heavily dependent on the sector in which you operate. For example, it is easier to generate conversions for a restaurant than for a webshop. Similarly, if you are active in a niche, you will also find it easier to achieve a high conversion rate.

What is a good conversion percentage? The following average figures are useful indicators:

- lower than 4% – poor result;
- 10% – good result;
- 15% or higher – excellent result.

Of course, the better you and your company are able to perform, the more customers you will be able to persuade and the more recommendations you will be able to convert into real sales. At Sunday, we have managed to achieve an average conversion rate of 56 percent, which is exceptionally high. It means that more than half of all the people who receive recommendations about us become our customers.

Recommendations can vary dramatically in quality. Sometimes, you will be recommended for a product or service at which you excel. On other occasions, you will be recommended for things that you are not good at or which you don't really want to do. If this latter eventuality happens too often, you need to consider giving your ambassadors more appropriate training. By showing them what, in your eyes, constitutes a top-class recommendation, you should be able to improve your conversion rate significantly.

Example

Ward runs a first-class decorating company, specialised in high-end finishing. Because his standard of quality is so high, he only works in the finest and most luxurious villas. Of course, his craftsmanship comes at a price, but you get what you pay for: if you want the best, you can't expect it to be cheap. Although his customers often recommend him, they know that he is unlikely to act on all of these recommendations. Painting a garden shed at a knock-down price is not worth it for him! Although his customers mean well, this kind of recommendation actually does little to help Ward or benefit his business. In fact, it can even have a counterproductive effect, because he has to keep on turning down all these low-end jobs, which may gain him a reputation of being 'difficult'.

Additional turnover per ambassador

Last but definitely not least, the additional revenue derived through the efforts of each ambassador is also very important. How much more have you been able to sell thanks to the recommendations of your biggest fans? Try to quantify and record this data as accurately as you can, not only for the purposes of your own internal marketing reporting, but also as a means to strengthen your relationship with your ambassadors. By sharing with them in a transparent manner the data that shows just how much their efforts on behalf of your company have raised, this will generate goodwill that will prompt them to continue or even to redouble those efforts in the future. Your ambassadors are your best friends and this how you want it to stay. Ambassadors who make good recommendations for you on an annual basis are worth their weight in gold.

Of course, monitoring this metric is also important for yourself. If you are taking the trouble to invest in ambassadors, you want to know how much you are getting back in return. If you have chosen to follow the ambassadorial pathway, it will fill you with pride to see this 'additional turnover' grow year after year. Pride in yourself, pride in your company and pride in your ambassadors.

Keeping the data

There are different ways that you can record and store the data relating to your ambassadors. The method you choose will largely depend on the size of your ambassador programme. At the beginning or in smaller companies, a clear Excel spreadsheet is often a good idea (see www.teamsunday.com/iedereen-superfan). This will allow you to fill in the various columns in the manner that seems most suitable. Once you have this raw data, you can then start drawing your own conclusions and accordingly making plans for the future.

As your ambassador programme expands, or in large and more complex companies, it will probably be necessary (and wiser) to use one of the CRM tools, like Teamleader, HubSpot or Salesforce. These tools will keep and classify all your data accurately, so that you can prepare advanced reports that will enable you to clarify and fine-tune your ambassador marketing strategy. For those who are interested in taking things a step further, there are even more sophisticated tools like Social Seeder, which are designed to measure ambassadorship digitally.

Whichever way you choose to collect and collate your data, the key to success is to always do it as accurately and as consistently as possible. If you learn that someone has made a recommendation for your company, record it properly – whether in a spreadsheet, a CRM system or something more state-of-the-art.

ACTION POINTS

If you want to invest more in ambassador marketing, you obviously need to know where, when and in which channels you can best make use of your marketing budget. The action points in this chapter are intended to allow you to establish your current position with clarity and accuracy. Which channels are you investing in at the moment? In which channels are you not yet active? Are you focusing primarily on trying to attract new customers or are you concentrating on the retention of your existing ones?

An important KPI in this respect is 'cost per newly acquired customer'. How much are you currently paying to attract each new customer in the various channels in which you operate? If, for example, you place an advertisement with a discount voucher in a local magazine, record accurately how many people use the voucher or contact you in response to the advert. Once you have this information, you should be able to establish how many of these customers are new. To determine the cost per new customer, simply divide the amount of your marketing costs by the number of new customers concerned:

Marketing costs / number of new customers = cost per new customer.

Example: If it costs you 500 euros to place an advert with a discount voucher in your local magazine and if the action eventually brings in eight new customers, your marketing costs per newly acquired customer amount to 62.50 euro (500 / 8).

Calculate the costs per new customer in this manner for every marketing channel in which you are active. In this way, you will be able to analyse your ambassador marketing campaign more objectively later on. The purpose of the ambassador marketing channel is to provide you with new customers at a cost that is lower than your current average cost. But you first need to know what this average cost currently is.

We are confident that in the long run ambassador marketing will provide you with a much better ROI than any of the other channels, but we also want your efforts in this direction to show more immediate results.

Make it a habit to ask new customers how they first got to hear about your company. There is a good chance that an ambassador will have had something to do with it. This simple technique will offer you two important benefits:

1   It will give you better data. Thanks to this information, you will be able to better assess the channels that are providing you with the most new customers. This, in turn, will allow you to better monitor your costs per customer per channel.

2   If you learn that new customers are being attracted by ambassadors, it gives you the opportunity to thank those ambassadors personally. In this way, your ambassadors will know that they are important to you, which will spur them on to make further recommendations. At the same time, new customers will also be made aware that recommendations are important to you, so that they might feel inclined to make recommendations of their own.

These new habits will have a much greater impact on your company than you might expect. You will discover via which channels your customers first learned about you and will also – and more importantly – be able to calculate the cost per customer per channel. This will allow you to decide whether or not to invest more or less budget in channels that are performing better or worse than expected. As a result, you will get a much clearer picture of which marketing actions are bringing you the biggest return and will also come to realise that ambassador marketing is already working hard on your behalf.

THE AMBASSADORS FOR YOUR COMPANY

'The more people you meet, and the more people you have influence over, the more your business can scale quicker.'

Peter Jones

Although you might not realise it, you almost certainly already have a number of ambassadors working on your behalf. These ambassadors can be divided up into different categories, which each have a different relationship with your company.

It is the intensity of the relationship that determines into which category they fall. The closer the relationship, the more effective their ambassadorship is likely to be. For example, you have a close relationship with the people who work in your company (employees or team members). As a result, they probably have the most potential to become proud ambassadors. They work hard each day to build up your company and its reputation. The second category consists of your customers and suppliers. They are directly influenced by how – and how successfully – your company performs. The third group is the wider public. This is a very broad group and can include people who have seen one of your adverts in a magazine, or live in the same town, or drive past your premises each day on the way to their own work. In general, members of the public do not have a personal relationship with your company, but this does not prevent them (or some of them) from giving you recommendations.

Your ambassadors represent a massive advantage for your company, in a number of different ways. In this chapter we will look at the three most important of these ways, where your superfans can really make a difference. Firstly, your ambassadors are able to influence people directly. A positive influence of this kind, particularly on stakeholders, usually leads to better business results. The department that is most sensitive to (and benefits most from) the effects of ambassadorship is the sales department. Ambassadors pave the way for your sales teams and help to boost your turnover. However, they also have a significant impact on your marketing department. The greater the number of people who talk positively about your company, the more well known it will become, which will also help to boost sales. No-one understands the value of ambassadorship better than the marketeers. A third but less obvious effect of your ambassadors will be felt in your HR department. Employer branding to recruit and (above all) keep new talent is now a key priority in fast-growing companies, and your ambassadors can make your company shine! In other words, ambassador marketing is the ideal channel to have a major positive impact on three of your most important departments.

There are also different ways in which your ambassadors can have an impact on your turnover. Making recommendations to new potential customers is the most obvious one. It is well known that customers who find their way to a company via a recommendation offer good prospects for a sale, and perhaps more than one. The more people recommend your company, the more 'warm' leads you will have and the more purchases they will be likely to make. However, another way in which ambassadors can boost your sales drive is by acting as internal champions. Even if they fail to generate new leads, some ambassadors can have a positive influence on the number of sales that are made.

MARKETING AND THE AWARENESS PHASE

Every sales process passes through three phases: the awareness phase, the consideration phase and the decision phase. Every potential customer has to negotiate each of these phases if he wants to make a purchase, not only in a B2B context but also with regard to individual 'private' purchases. In the awareness phase you want to let people know that your company exists and that you have a solution for their problem or need. Of course, you want to spread this message to as many people as possible and also as cheaply as possible.

You are probably already familiar with the various marketing techniques that are used to guide people into and through this awareness phase. You can adopt a broad approach with TV and online advertising or you can opt for a niche approach with attendance at specific trade fairs. However, the most powerful channel in this phase are your ambassadors. They can make potential new customers aware of your existence in the most natural and most effective manner of all. Converting satisfied customers into ambassadors will therefore ensure that they advertise your company time after time, guaranteeing a constant influx of potential new customers during the awareness phase.

A good example of this is the CrossFit story.

EVERYONE CROSSFIT

CrossFit is a popular form of fitness training, developed in the United States by Greg Glassman. On the one hand, CrossFit is a philosophy that rejects specialisation in one specific discipline (regarding this as too one-dimensional), but at the same time it is also a competitive sport. In the US, CrossFit games and championships, in which many thousands of people take part, are organised each year. This enthusiastic community is extremely important for CrossFit. Everyone in America (and often now in other countries) knows someone who does CrossFit and these CrossFitters like nothing better than to talk about their new sport to whoever will listen. As a result, almost every CrossFitter is an ambassador, creating a snowball effect of new members, who in turn also become ambassadors.

Thanks in large part to these ambassadors, CrossFit has spread virally around the world. Although the company was only started as recently as 2000, there are now more than 15,000 CrossFit clubs worldwide and most people have now at the very least heard about the concept. Equally impressive is the fact that CrossFit has achieved this global conquest relatively cheaply. This was only made possible by the power of its ambassadors, who, irrespective of age, profession or physical condition, all wanted to get fit as quickly as possible and then encouraged others to do the same.

A number of sportswear brands following in the wake of CrossFit also successfully played the ambassadorship card and developed sophisticated ambassadorial programmes. In the world of sport, ambassadorship is based on a mutual sense of responsibility. The ambassador feels responsible towards the new sporting beginner/member and puts his reputation on the line to attract the 'newbie'. In return, this new 'customer/starter' does not want to disappoint the ambassador and this increases his commitment to persist and to follow the guidance given by the ambassador.

The awareness phase is frequently the most expensive phase of the sales process for a company and its marketing department, because it is usually necessary to reach out to a very broad potential target group. What's more, it is often a target group that does not yet know your company, so that your marketing message fails to set any bells of recognition ringing. The best way to change all this is with ambassadors. Nothing and no-one is better than ambassadors at quickly, convincingly and cheaply interesting potential customers/members during the awareness phase. Every time an ambassador speaks to someone about his passion, this means that at the very least one new person has become familiar with your company. And it costs you nothing. Moreover, in many cases it does not stop there, but pushes people on into the consideration and decision phases. This was the basis of CrossFit's success and it is a model that you can see used by leading companies in many different sectors: Apple, Zara, Sriracha & Spanx, to name but a few. They all allow their ambassadors to do their marketing for them. As a result, they even manage to save money on their traditional marketing budget.

FOMO AT ZARA

Zara spends just 0.3 percent of its turnover on advertising, while most of its competitors spend an average of 3.5 percent. How is this possible? In Zara's case, it is the result of a number of far-reaching decisions and strategies implemented in recent years, such as 'Be Fast, Not First', through which Zara is able to offer affordable copies of high-end fashion brands. Ambassadorship plays an important role in this process. Zara listens constantly to its customers. When a customer makes it known that he/she hates or loves a particular product, this information is never ignored, but instead is recorded and considered when new decisions need to be made. Zara also focuses heavily on word-of -mouth advertising as the best way to keep the brand top-of-mind.

Another of Zara's smart tactics is to only offer a limited number of each new item, so that it creates a sense of urgency or 'fear of missing out' (FOMO) amongst its customers As a result, when Zara customers succeed in buying the very latest products that they have set their heart on, it makes them feel as though they belong to some kind of exclusive club. In most cases, it also means that they want to show off their new 'trophy' to all their family and friends. The majority of Instagram posts that mention Zara are not created by the company or by its paid influencers (although it does use them – see below) but by ordinary members of the public. In this way, Zara is perceived by the followers of these members of the public as being a true high-end fashion brand. If you realise that Zara has more than 27 million followers on Instagram, it is not difficult to see why every social media action dreamt up by the company soon takes off and starts leading a life of its own!

Because the truth is, of course, that Zara does engage in marketing; in fact, quite a lot of it.[8] However, the intelligent tactics used by the company are often not regarded as 'traditional' marketing, so that it takes place under the radar, as a result of which it does not come across as being hard, 'in-your-face' marketing.

As mentioned, Zara does indeed work together with influencers to create content and generate name recognition with a new young public, but the media value of these paid collaborations represents just 1 percent of the company's social media value. In other words, the vast majority of the value created by Zara's presence on social media is created organically by ambassadors and fans, who communicate independently about the brand.

This is all comes back to the fact that Zara offers quality products in relatively limited amounts, which stimulates its fan base to 'boast' about the fact that they have actually managed to acquire the blouse, shirt or trousers of their dreams in the very latest style. This not only encourages envy, but also emulation. It likewise underlines the fact that Zara's business model is its strongest marketing tactic.

THE CONSIDERATION PHASE: IS THIS REALLY SOMETHING FOR ME?

In the awareness phase your ambassadors create volume: the more people they address, the more potential customers enter into your sales funnel. Once people have learnt about your company, the next step is to guide them into the consideration phase. How can you persuade customers to consider the solution that your company is offering them? The answer: ambassadors. In this phase, the testimonies and recommendations of your ambassadors are a powerful tool. According to a worldwide study conducted by Nielsen,[9] 84 percent of consumers claim to have more confidence in the recommendations of family and friends than in any other marketing channel. In other words, by investing in your ambassadors you will be investing in the strongest and most reliable marketing option.

During the consideration phase, people are on the look-out for more information about your company and the solution you are proposing for their problem. At the same time, they will probably also investigate other alternatives. The key to success in this phase is therefore to be seen as the best, most reliable and most recommended of all the available solutions. You must persuade them that your company is best positioned to help them and that your product or service is what they really need.

Potential customers are bombarded daily with information (or, to give it its proper name, advertising). Your competitors will be trying everything they know to persuade people not to choose your company, but to choose theirs instead. They will put adverts in the media or folders in letter boxes, organise promotional events, conduct market surveys, etc. In this struggle for the attention of potential customers, the direct recommendations of your ambassadors can make a crucial difference.

THE DECISION PHASE: YOUR CHAMPIONS AT WORK

In a B2B context, ambassadors can make a huge difference in the decision phase. Will the purchase go through or will the customer opt for one of your rivals? During complex negotiations between companies, it is often necessary for a number of people to give their approval before a deal can be clinched. For this reason, it is a good idea for you as the selling company to have an ambassador or two in the buying company, if at all possible. They can ensure that your interests will be defended in internal discussions and will push you forward as the best possible business partner.

The influence and reputation of these 'internal champions' can make all the difference between winning and losing a deal. So if you are lucky enough or smart enough to have internal champions of this kind, make sure you treat them well. If you can keep them on your side, over time they will give your products, services and solutions the push they need, not only at their present employers, but also at any future ones. These ambassadors can operate at all levels of your potential customer's company: sales, administration, HR, etc. They can argue your cause from any of these positions.

The moral of the previous few pages? People who are your fans and who are therefore willing and able to serve as your ambassadors can exercise crucial influence on all three phases of the sales process.

Remember, however, that ambassadors can also be early warning stations when things look like they are going wrong. If they tell you that your products and services are not up to the mark as a solution in a particular situation, you would be well advised to listen to them.

Bearing in mind the Zara model described above, it is clear that ambassadorship can work in both directions. If you fail to keep your customers happy, they will not talk about you or may even talk about you negatively, which will have a lasting negative effect in the future. Even the biggest marketing budget in the world would find it hard to break this negative spiral. Make sure, then, that your customers are satisfied and say good things about your products and services. It will make the sales process so much easier for you! Oscar Wilde once said: 'There is only one thing in life worse than being talked about and that is not being talked about'. But in a business context that is only true if all that talk is positive.

SUNKEN, ELEVATED OR NATURAL? CHOOSING A SWIMMING POOL

The third blisteringly hot summer in a row. Soon even ex-president Trump will find it hard to deny that climate change is here to stay. The temperature has been above 30°C for weeks, with no end in sight. And it looks almost certain that next year will be the same. To plan for this eventuality, Tom and Danielle, the parents of two teenage daughters, plan to invest in a swimming pool. After an evening of fruitful family discussion around the dining table, they agree that there are two possible solutions.

The first option is an 'elevated' above-ground swimming pool. This is the cheapest option but adds nothing (or very little) to the value of their house as a whole. The second option is a sunken swimming pool set into the ground. Of course, this is pricey, but it would yield a clear added value. To give themselves time to think things through, the family agree to hold a second council of war a week later, to decide which of the two options to pursue.

However, when this second meeting starts, the oldest daughter suggests a possible third solution. She has heard from a girl in her class how happy she is with the swimming pond her family installed a few years ago. In the winter, it serves as an attractive water feature in their garden. In the summer, it is great to just pop into the water to cool off. What's more, the concept is very ecologically responsible. After a brief discussion, Tom, Danielle and the girls agree that this third option is actually not a bad idea and is broadly in keeping with what they want, and at a price they can afford.

Prior to this, the family had not been aware that a swimming pond was an option. In other words, they were not yet in the awareness phase. In this story, the classmate of the oldest daughter therefore acted as an ambassador for swimming ponds. It is thanks to her that the family has now moved into the awareness phase.

Understandably, Tom and Danielle decide to do some further research about swimming ponds. They use Google to find a list of local contractors, read online blogs and send off for various relevant brochures. They are now in the consideration phase and want to find out everything they can about swimming ponds and the people who install them.

They soon discover that there is a veritable mountain of information on this subject. So much, in fact, that it is very difficult to make a decision. Every company they contact says that their approach, materials, personnel, etc. are the best! Objective information is hard to find. To try and help them forward, they ask their oldest daughter if her classmate would put them in touch with her parents. They have had a swimming pond for the past two years, so should be able to say something meaningful about the various pros and cons. On the phone, these parents, Peter and Tina, confirm that they, like their daughter, are also very happy with their swimming pond. You can jump in to cool off whenever you like, whilst at the same time encouraging greater biodiversity in your garden. They also mention that they were very impressed with [Company X], who installed their pond. The concept was creative, the planning was perfect and everything was completed on time and within budget. What more could you wish for?

Now that Tom, Danielle and the girls are in the consideration phase, they go in search of as much objective and correct information as they can find. Because consumer recommendations are generally regarded as the most reliable form of information, they decide to seek contact with people who already have a swimming pond. At this stage, [Company X] has a huge lead over its competitors, thanks to the comments made by the parents of the eldest daughter's classmate. Because these comments were so positive, there is a good chance that Tom and Danielle will now decide to contact this company.

This story illustrates the power of ambassadors in two different phases of the sales funnel. It shows that customers can be strongly influenced at different moments in the sales process by superfans who push their favourite company, product, service, solution, etc. Do you recognise yourself in this story? How often have you asked people for advice when you are planning to buy something that you really know nothing about? Installing a new bathroom? Booking a restaurant in a town where you have never been? The best bank to take out a loan? Every day we all need to search for what we regard as objective and reliable information, so that we can make the right decisions. Companies that have ambassadors who are willing to talk about them positively are in pole position in the race to win the customer's favour.

Of course, this can also work in the opposite direction. What if Peter and Tina had said that they can never swim in their pond, because the water is always dirty? And that [Company X] has done nothing about it, notwithstanding their repeated complaints? In these circumstances, would Tom and Danielle consider contacting [Company X], even for moment? What do you think?

APPLYING FOR A JOB: JUST LIKE BUYING AND SELLING

You can compare applying for and starting a new job with one of the biggest purchasing decisions in your life. It is one of the most crucial decisions you will ever make, so you need to get it right. Like making a major purchase (house, car, etc.), you will conduct a thorough information search in advance, to make sure that there is a good match between what you want and what is on offer. As a result, most job seekers are very well informed about the companies where they apply to work. After all, with a little bit of effort there are plenty of useful sources of information that you can tap: current employees, former employees, past job applicants, suppliers, other stakeholders, etc. Each of these groups will have an opinion about the company.

What is the situation on the other side of the interview table? It can often be difficult for employers to find and bind the right employees, especially when the economy is doing well or if you are in a sector where there is a shortage of trained personnel. This explains why many companies now invest time, energy and resources in employer branding, in the hope that they can stay one step ahead of their rivals in the race for talent. Good employers get noticed, appeal to the imagination and work like a magnet. In this respect, proud, committed and motivated employees are the very best ambassadors for your company. These are people who feel truly at home in the organisation, give the best of themselves every day and know how they can contribute to the organisation's mission and vision. People who work hard day after day to make good their employer's promises to its demanding customers. In this way, every employee can be a key player in helping to secure customer satisfaction and improving the long term image of the organisation. So how does this help you to recruit and retain the very best people? The key to success lies in efficient and effective communication by the HR department throughout the entire trajectory of the employee journey. This is a journey that starts even before a candidate applies for a job and doesn't even finish after he has left the company, usually many years later.

Every step of the employee journey is a step in which ambassadors (whether internal or external) play a role: from the moment when the candidate applicant becomes aware of the existence of the company until the moment when he retires and looks back happily on his time with his former employer, as a result of which he is now prepared to recommend that same employer to others.

What would it be like if everyone who is currently employed by your company or had ever worked for you in the past was super-positive about what you do and talked to everyone about how they feel? What if people who are asking around for tips about a good potential employer are constantly hearing your name? How easy or difficult do you think it would be in these circumstances to attract the best talent for your team? Anyone who knows how much recruitment costs will also know that using your own staff as your ambassadors offers by far the biggest ROI.

The three phases of the sales funnel have their equivalents when someone is searching for a new job. First, there is a need for awareness: a candidate has to know that your company exists before he can make his application. Here your ambassadors can help: you don't want to leave things to chance and just hope that the candidate finds his way to your job page. During the consideration phase, he will collect information from different sources, including your ambassadors, about the culture within your company, before he eventually decides whether to submit his application or not. In the decision phase, he will make a final decision between your company and two or three others he has also been considering. Having the right ambassadors will ensure that you are the one he picks, so that you can look forward to welcoming another strong member to your team.

Once he is on board, you can start training him to become a new ambassador for your company in his own right. With this in mind, make sure that you have a good onboarding programme for new employees (and also for interns), so that the 'newbies' immediately get a positive vibe from working for you. To cement this good first impression, also create a pleasing working environment that will make your people feel at home and continue to convince them that they have, indeed, made the right choice. This means that your organisational culture must be pleasant, efficient and transparent in a manner that stimulates and rewards excellent performance.

Nowadays, employees are often more critical, more empowered and more enterprising than in the past. This requires a deepening of the relationship with the employer, in which greater interaction is essential. This means involving your employees actively in the things for which your company stands. Leave space for dialogue and self-interpretation. In this way, the employee will be able to put the story of your company into practice in a shape and form for which he is partly responsible. This will make him all the more willing to talk to others about who you are and what you do.

When an employee has the possibility to grow and develop within an organisation (for example, through structured training), he will feel appreciated and involved, which will further increase his commitment. These are highly useful ways to stimulate the creation of good ambassadors. Even when the time comes for the employee to leave the organisation, investing in a good offboarding pathway usually reaps its rewards. You want the employee to leave your company with a good feeling, so that he will continue to be prepared to say good things about you.

Up-to-date companies that wish to achieve all the above objectives set up quite sophisticated programmes for the purpose (this is known as employee advocacy), because experience has shown that the results can be spectacular.

A survey carried out by medium.com revealed that 79 percent of companies were of the opinion that such programmes had increased their general visibility (awareness), while 65 percent concluded that their brand was more easily recognised and 44 percent noted an increase in web activity (inbound) as a result of pure employee advocacy.

It is also important to bear in mind that all your employees have their own online and offline network. The average user of online media has 338 Facebook friends (source: Pew Research Center) and 930 LinkedIn connections (source: medium. com). If we add to this hundreds of other WhatsApp and Instagram contacts, it soon becomes clear that each and every member of your workforce has an average potential reach of something like 2,000 people!

Last but not least, it is worth mentioning that ambassadorship can also work to the benefit of the 'mini-company' that every individual job applicant represents. Candidates also need people who are willing to tell potential future employers just how good they are. After all, who would you recruit: someone you know nothing about or someone who has a glowing recommendation? No brainer.

BOL.COM

Bol.com is the largest (and still expanding) webshop in the Benelux. The company was founded in 1999 by the German media concern Bertelsmann AG and has its headquarters in Utrecht, in The Netherlands. After just a decade in business, the company had more than 1,800 employees and offered more than 33 million articles for sale over the internet. In addition to its large permanent workforce, bol.com is continually on the look-out for temporary employees to help them to deal with peak sales periods like Black Friday, Christmas and New Year. To thank all its personnel for how hard they had worked during these super-busy periods, the company recently decided that it wanted to give everyone a reward. But what, exactly?

Together with a creative external agency, the Dutch team at bol.com came up with the idea of gifting every employee a pair of warm slippers with the company logo, so that they could put their feet up and relax after all the hard work they had done. These bol.com slippers were immediately a big hit and soon became a hype within the company. The combination of a cool and contemporary brand (bol.com) with an everyday (and some might even say 'old-fashioned') product like a pair of slippers was a stroke of genius. So much so that the slippers are now something of a collector's item!

© Sunday

Photos on social media and in the company's internal WhatsApp groups show how the slippers are still used on a daily basis by employees when they are at home. This helps to cement bol.com in a positive way in both their hearts and minds. Which, as a company, is precisely what you need if you want to create first-class ambassadors for you and your brand.

EVERY DEPARTMENT CAN BENEFIT FROM AMBASSADORS

As you have been able to read in this chapter, every department in your organisation can benefit from a strong ambassador marketing strategy. Your ambassadors can attract new customers and even new employees, as well as persuading them to stay with you. For example, it is possible for an ambassador in a single conversation to recommend your products to a potential buyer and your company to a potential new recruit. What's more, this happens 24 hours a day and seven days a week, albeit in a highly unprogrammed and unpredictable manner. That being said, if you play your cards right, you can help to perpetuate this unstructured promotion of your company for several years at a time. All it takes is a relatively modest investment in your ambassadors and the development of a programme that will guide them in the right direction and show them appreciation for what they have done. Ambassador programmes are powerful levers that will save you huge amounts of time and resources in the future, repaying your basic investment many times over. The following graphic illustrates how subjects are perceived by the public in relation to the people who talk about them. The figures show clearly that what is said by an internal ambassador (employee advocacy) is nearly always regarded as being more reliable than interventions by other (and supposedly more 'expert') stakeholders, such as the CEO, or a plug by a media figure. No further comment is required...

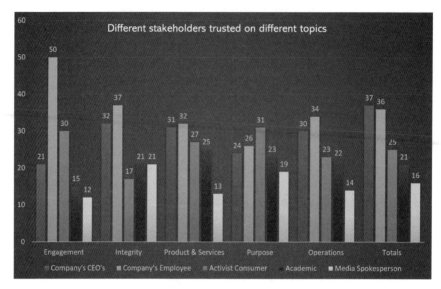

© Edelman trust barometer 2014

'Clothes mean nothing until someone lives in them.'

Marc Jacobs

SUMUP

SumUp is a super-fast-growing international fintech company, first founded in Berlin in 2012. Today, it already has more than 2,000 employees, but continues to attract roughly a dozen new ones each month. Perhaps it is no surprise, then, that the company is currently the market leader in MPOSM. In what? MPOSM stands for Mobile Point of Sale Machine; in other words, the payment terminals that you find in shops and catering outlets. At SumUp, they are passionately convinced that everyone must be given the opportunity to start their own business, if that is what they want. To make this possible, they provide small businesses with powerful tools for the running of their companies. They regard the success of their customers as their own success.

Because of SumUp's rapid rate of growth, with new recruits arriving almost every week, the company has decided that it seriously needs to strengthen its internal and external branding, so that it can create a close-knit community both in and around the company. SumUp merchandising plays an important role in this process, since it supports three of the key pillars detailed in the SumUp mission statement:

© lifesasumup.com

1   External branding. SumUp often takes part in business events. At these events, it wants its people to be readily identifiable by their identical but fashionably cool clothing, which not only makes a clear statement about the company culture, but is also intended to trigger and motivate new people who know nothing about the company. The old adage says that you only get one chance to make a first impression, and SumUp wants to make a super-good first impression.

2   Internal branding. Trainees and new recruits are issued with their SumUp clothing on day one of their employment, which ensures that the brand and the culture it represents immediately become a part of their life.

© Sunday

3   Building a community. All the employees at SumUp, whether temporary
    or permanent, can recognise each other instantly, so that they feel a strong
    connection as a result. SumUppers – as they like to call themselves – are a
    group of motivated people, who all have the same objective and are proud
    of it!

For many, the SumUp hoodies are the recognisable symbol of how new
and not-so-new team members are working together under a single flag.
SumUppers can even recognise each other during their free time, because
many of them wear their hoodies then as well...

ACTION POINTS

Being aware of the positive impact that ambassadors can have on your organisation is already a huge step in the right direction. There are plenty of concrete action points that can help you to produce results quickly with your ambassadors. Here are some practical tips to increase the value of your ambassadors in the different phases of the sales funnel.

Awareness

- Ensure that your ambassadors have an interesting and preferably entertaining story to tell about your company. Nobody is going to get excited by 'Company X offers the best value for money'. You need something warmer, more human and more amusing than that! The better the story, the more inclined your ambassadors will be to repeat it. The story can be about anything, as long as it touches a chord: the path you have followed as an entrepreneur, or how you created something unique, or even how you sent a block of cheese into space (which is the story of the Groendal cheese farm in Flanders, which supplies cheese to NASA astronauts – tgroendal.be).
- Provide your ambassadors with any marketing material that you might have available. Even if you have nothing more than visitor cards, give them some. These cards will trigger them to talk about you.

Consideration

- Help your ambassadors to develop the right reflexes. What problems do your solutions solve? What signals can they look for in potential customers? Train them how to recognise these signals and link them to the solutions you are proposing. Are you selling drills? Teach them how to search for people who may need to make holes...
- Provide your ambassadors with an open communication channel, so that when they spot an opportunity, they can get in touch with your company quickly, easily and confidentially. Eliminate any friction in the communication process that might hinder them from contacting you when they need to.

Conversion

- Keep your ambassadors 'in the loop'. Let them know the results of their efforts. Show appreciation for what they have done. Build up a relationship of trust. The more you can involve them in all aspects of what you do, the more willing they will be to keep on pushing new potential customers in your direction.
- Suggest to the ambassadors where they can best talk with potential new customers and also what they might like to say. Your ambassadors are the best possible advocates for your cause and are best positioned to remove any doubts that new customers might still have.

Using your ambassadors wisely during the different phases of the decision-making process can make all the difference.

CHAPTER 5

DEVELOPING YOUR AMBASSADOR MARKETING

AN AMBASSADOR MARKETING STRATEGY: ADDING PEOPLE TO YOUR TRIBE

There are two ways your company can grow: organic growth or strategic growth.

Organic growth is the more spontaneous way of growing. You keep on attracting customer after customer and assume that your most satisfied customers will become ambassadors. As a result, you will have a new crop of ambassadors each year, without really doing very much to acquire them or to keep them sweet. It all happens automatically. Recommendations continue to be made, albeit in a random and unpredictable way. There is no programme for your ambassadors, no structure in what they do, and you make little or no investment to change a situation with which you are generally satisfied.

Most companies are happy to breeze along in this unstructured manner. They know that recommendations are one of the best forms – if not the best form – of advertising, but they are still unwilling to invest in a programme to attract even more ambassadors. 'Why should we?' they often say. 'It will happen anyway, like it always has in the past.' These companies see ambassadors as a natural by-product of the quality of what they sell. And, to some extent, they are right. As a result, ambassador marketing is not always taken seriously as a real communication and marketing channel. However, there is also a different, more efficient and altogether better way of dealing with your ambassadors. This is the strategic growth approach.

Strategic growth means dealing in a smarter and more structured way with the potential of your ambassadors. We have seen in the previous chapters that there are different ways to have an impact on your fans. Once you start measuring your ambassador cohort and its effects, you can also start to test ideas to improve their ROI. By making the acquisition and use of new ambassadors a strategic objective, you can achieve better and faster results than if you simply rely on organic growth. By devoting time, energy and money to your ambassador marketing programme, you will accelerate the expansion of your company.

In this chapter we will look at the ways in which you can develop an ambassador marketing programme step by step and how you can make the influence of your ambassadors even more powerful and efficient. This can be done by using the so-called DEAL framework, which embraces the key factors on which you can work to improve the performance and return of your super-fans. DEAL stands for Develop, Engage, Attract and Love. By focusing on and investing in these factors, you can significantly heighten the strategic impact of your ambassador marketing channel. What does such a DEAL programme involve? Read on, and all will be revealed.

THE DEAL FRAMEWORK

The DEAL framework is a schedule that is often used in HR settings, but with a few minor adjustments it can be usefully employed for all the different stakeholders in your company. By focusing on the framework's constituent pillars, you can improve the performance of your ambassadors on all fronts.

Maker's Mark ambassadors[10]

Maker's Mark is an American producer of small batch bourbon whiskey in the town of Loretto, Kentucky. Maker's Mark is easily recognised by its square-shaped bottles, which are sealed with red wax. The distillery is part of the American Whiskey Trail and the Kentucky Bourbon Trail. Yet notwithstanding this impressive track record, Maker's Mark actually excels at something completely different: its ambassadors' programme.

The Maker's Mark® Ambassador Program (American spelling!) must be one of the most well-considered and deeply developed programmes of its kind anywhere in the world. As Bill Samuels Jr., the company's very first ambassador, puts it: 'Maker's Mark was built on friends telling friends about our delicious, full-flavoured bourbon. I'd love for you to join me in continuing that tradition.' Mr Samuels is now the Chairman Emeritus of Maker's Mark.

New ambassadors are 'allocated' their own individual barrel of Maker's Mark® and their names are engraved on a special board that is then attached to it. After five years of ripening, the ambassadors can then buy exclusive whiskey from their very 'own' barrel, with their name on the bottle label. As you might imagine, for real fans this is a unique experience.

In their communication, the company talks quite openly about the 'responsibilities' of its ambassadors, which include introducing friends and family to Maker's Mark. In this way, the brand has taken ambassadorship and word-of-mouth advertising to the next level. Their programme makes use of many of the tactics you have already read about in this book:

- establishing a personal connection with the ambassadors;
- offering exclusive access to things not available to non-ambassadors;
- establishing clear identification with the concept of ambassadorship and underlining its importance for the future growth of the company;
- integrating ambassadors into the company's community and vision.

Of course, you cannot become a Maker's Mark ambassador just like that. The first step is an online quiz, which tests whether or not you know enough about the brand to be considered. Only the successful candidates are allowed to join the Maker's Mark® Ambassador Program, and are given an official certificate to prove it!

Develop

This pillar focuses on the development and training of your ambassadors. The more familiar they are with your products and services, the better and more appropriately they can recommend those products and services to others. Similarly, the more they know about your company, the more they will be willing to talk about it. Remember also that it is important for your ambassadors to know who you regard as your ideal customers and what you regard as your ideal deal. This will help to ensure that there is a good match between the people they recommend and what you are able to offer. By training your fans properly, you will help them to tell better and more interesting stories. Of course, a good ambassador will also want to know that the people to whom he recommends your company are also satisfied with the end result. This is not only good for their own ambassadorial reputation, but also makes it more likely that the satisfied new customer will also start making recommendations to others. This is known as the 'pay it forward' principle.

The development of an ambassadors' programme is a marathon, not a sprint. Ambassadors are not (usually) members of staff who you can send off for an intensive training course, whether they like it or not. No, because your ambassadors are volunteers, it is necessary to give them guidance and training in a manner that they will enjoy. One option is give them a kind of 'light' version of the training that you give to your sales team, which deals with the following themes:

- product and service range;
- ideal customer profile;
- advantages in relation to the competition;
- monitoring procedures for the recommendations.

As far as possible, your ambassadors should always be kept informed about the most recent new additions to your range. For a butcher, it is important that your ambassadors can tell people that you now offer a ready-to-eat-tapas board. For a car brand, they can tell their network all about your latest new model. By keeping your ambassadors fully in the picture, you ensure that their knowledge is up-to-date and also further stimulate their engagement. You can do this, for example, by inviting them to attend exclusive online or offline events for new product launches. This not only gives them a pleasant evening, but also the chance to see the new product first hand. At the same time, you can ask your sales team to further 'train' the ambassadors, as far as the circumstances allow.

In the film world, the producers and directors of new films make use of what is known as 'sneak previews'. A sneak preview was originally the showing of a film before its official release for public viewing. Sometimes, the invited audience didn't even know in advance what they would be watching.

Today, the purpose of the sneak preview is not only to test how the new film will be received by the public, but also to establish for which target group the film is most suited, and also to generate the necessary word-of-mouth advertising. If a group of mega-influencers (super-ambassadors) are given a sneak preview, there is a very strong likelihood that they will want to tell everyone they know ('Do you know what I've seen?'), so that positive communication about the film – the so-called 'buzz around'– can be set in motion.

The term sneak preview is now used in many other fields but the basic principle remains the same: a limited public is allowed to get privileged access to a new product before its official launch. For example, the Dutch fun park Efteling, in collaboration with Nickelodeon, organised a competition for which the prize was a sneak preview of their new 'George and the Dragon' attraction. The winners were allowed to be the first members of the public to test the attraction, which made them feel special, chosen and appreciated. These are three very good emotions for creating new ambassadors.

Ideal customer profile

Attracting the right customers is crucial for any company. For this reason, it is important that you provide your ambassadors with a clear profile of the ideal customers for your company. Are you looking for customers within a radius of five kilometres (a company that sees proximity as one of its trump cards)? Or are you interested in people with adventurous hobbies (a company that sells off-road vehicles). It is a good idea to spread this ideal customer profile via different marketing channels. This is possible, for example, through a testimonial or by creating a buyer persona. The more information your ambassadors possess about your ideal customer, the more likely it is that they will recommend your company to the right people. A video can also be a short and powerful tool to share this information.

Advantages in relation to the competition

What makes your company different from all the others? Why do people buy your products and not those of your biggest competitor? This is something that every company will know, but this information is not always passed on to its ambassadors. This is a mistake. You need to help your ambassadors to understand why they need to send customers to you and not to someone else. If your ambassadors are fully aware of your strong points, they can mention them in their conversations with potential new customers. If you have the fastest delivery or the best quality, they can share this information with their network. This will help them to avoid making 'bad' recommendations – for example, to customers who are only interested in the cheapest – and allow them to select the best playing field for the sales conversation to take place.

Monitoring procedures for the recommendations

If someone recommends your company to a friend, he wants to know that his friend will be in good hands if he decides to do business with you. There is nothing worse for an ambassador than to hear that someone to whom he made a recommendation later had a bad experience as a result. It is important that you remove this element of doubt from the situation by explaining clearly to your ambassadors how their recommendations will be monitored, step by step. Do you have an internal service that will provide follow-up within 24 hours? Or is it the boss who personally monitors recommendations, instead of a team member? Make your ambassadors feel confident that their recommendations will be tracked at a high level. Share the necessary information with them and study it closely yourself. With longer sales cycles, it can also be a good idea to provide your ambassadors with feedback in stages. You can do this in personal conversations or by creating a dedicated webpage, on which you can detail how the recommendation is being dealt with in each phase of the sales process.

Platforms for training your ambassadors

There are several different ways to give guidance and training to your ambassadors. We have already mentioned the organisation of exclusive events, where your sales team can give them subtle tips and hints to steer them in the right direction. However, you can also set up a closed Facebook or LinkedIn group to which all your ambassadors belong. This means that they will not only have contact with your company but also with each other, which will strengthen their sense of community and engagement. If you want to take this a stage further, you can also build this community into your official company website. By regularly interacting with your ambassadors in different ways, both online and offline, you gradually get closer and closer to them. These regular contact moments are the ideal opportunity for communicating new information, so that your biggest and best fans remain fully in the picture.

Lego Ideas[11]

Lego Ideas is one of the very best examples of ambassador marketing. Via the online Lego platform, it is possible for Lego fanatics to submit their own designs to the company. These designs are then assessed by the other users of the platform for a 'make or break' decision. The idea is that a good design, which may be used later, is first approved by the full Lego community. Of course, if a design is eventually put into production, this is the supreme accolade for a Lego enthusiast.

The online platform serves two main purposes for Lego. Firstly, it gives a boost (both psychological and numerical) to the Lego-Lovers community and provides them with more contact moments with the company. Adding an online element to a physical toy creates a better bond with the brand and also between the platform's users. This platform is the place where Lego ambassadors can meet each other and can discover new ways to interact with their favourite pastime. Secondly, it is a very useful tool for the company to collect and analyse all the information and ideas that exist within the Lego community, for the purpose of deciding which sets can be commercialised successfully in the future. In this respect, Lego Ideas is a classic example of co-creation between a company and its ambassadors.

Is a dedicated platform for your ambassadors taking things a bit too far in your case? If so, using a dedicated and exclusive newsletter can be a good alternative. This costs very little and can easily be done using a free online tool like Mailchimp. By circulating a newsletter intended exclusively for your ambassadors, you remain in direct communication with your biggest fans. What's more, you can use a newsletter to cover a variety of topics. In the early days of your ambassador marketing, this newsletter will probably be fairly short. But as the number of your ambassadors grows, you can systematically increase its length and its impact, providing information of a wide range of subjects that can include:

- sneak previews for new product releases;
- calls for the testing of new products;
- discount codes that are only made available to ambassadors;
- member-gets-member actions;
- 'a look behind the scenes' articles;
- exclusive events for ambassadors;
- press releases;
- limited editions.

You can set your own publication frequency for your newsletter. Monthly or quarterly are the most popular options. Be aware that too much communication can be regarded by some people as stalking. Keep the content of your newsletter fresh and varied. The more personal and unique items you are able to add, the more special and the more involved your ambassadors will feel.

Active ambassadors are worth their weight in gold and therefore deserve to receive graduation merchandise. Provide them with unique items that emphasise their engagement and its value to the company. For example, you can gift them an exclusive hoodie or t-shirt, which they will no doubt wear with pride. This will not only motivate them to become even more active on your behalf, but will also provide them with physical tools to advertise your company in public.

Engage

The more information you provide to your ambassadors, the more engagement you will get in return. More engagement means that your ambassadors will think about you more often, talk about you more often and make more repeat recommendations. As a result, more engagement means a bigger return for your company, which is obviously good. However, there are also other things that you can do to boost this engagement, in addition to giving your ambassadors the right information. In essence, engagement is based on three main pillars: communication, recognition and pleasure.

Communicate your mission and vision. The more you communicate with your ambassadors, the more involved they will feel with your company and brand. But be careful how you do it: for example, it is not a good idea to constantly bombard them with promotional offers or useless information. Most of your ambassadors will have an emotional connection with your company and brand, a connection that is often based on something more than factors like 'excellent value for money' or 'superior quality'. No, they are attracted to your company because of the things it represents and the values for which it stands. In their own way, they want to become (and are) a part of your team. They share the same mission and vision as you do, and they want to contribute towards their successful realisation. For example, brands like Tesla and Nike have a huge group of 'followers', who believe whole-heartedly in the aims and objectives of the company. But you don't have to be a large multinational to create this same effect.

Sunday has had ambassadors for years. For most of these early pioneers, the company's story was the most important factor in their fandom. They were fascinated by the journey of two friends from Roeselare who, in spite of their lack of money, experience and business connections, were able to build up an international company with major international customers like Google and Facebook. It is, indeed, a story that appeals to the imagination, but it was also a story that gave Sunday the kind of 'underdog' status that appeals to many people. When people apply for jobs with the company, they often tell us how they were amazed by the fact that everything started in the front room of Steven's parents' house. Of course, there is more to Sunday than just a good story. Our clear vision on ecological and ethical matters, our decision to confine our production to Europe and our desire to become a major player on the world stage has also helped to win us countless ambassadors over the years. These people want to support us in the pursuit of our goals, in part because they share them and in part because they appeal to sentiments that go far beyond pure sales talk about price and quality.

Conclusion? Make sure that your ambassadors know what you stand for and what impact you want to make in the world. This will make it easier to forge an emotional connection with them. No matter how small its impact to begin with, a good (and well-told) story will always continue to attract people. Whether it is an ice-cream parlour that only makes use of milk from local cows or a fitness chain that wants to make sport affordable for everyone, every story has the power to affect us. If you are not sure about the best way to project your own story, ask your current ambassadors what they say about you to others. What is it about your company that so appeals to them and why are they so keen to recommend you? You will probably be (pleasantly) surprised by some of the things you hear; often it is the smallest details that make the biggest difference.

In addition to having a good story to motivate them, it is also important to give your ambassadors due recognition for the efforts they make on your behalf. Everyone likes to get a pat on the back for what they have done, and ambassadors are no different. These people are putting their own reputation on the line by recommending your company, so the very least you can do is to thank them. There are different ways you can do this. Approaching them in person is always best, but this is not always practical once their numbers begin to grow significantly. Two other options that work well and are most appreciated by ambassadors is listening sincerely to what they have to say and rewarding them spontaneously with unexpected gifts.

The key words here are 'spontaneously' and 'unexpected'. You must avoid creating a 'you scratch my back' scenario, where rewards become almost automatic, since this will remove all spontaneity from your ambassadorship programme, which will seriously damage its credibility.

Listening to your ambassadors is also something you can do in different ways, and your choice will often depend on the sector in which you operate. Feedback panels are one of the strongest and most effective ways. Every time that Sunday develops a new product, structural feedback is requested from the company's ambassadors. For instance, they will be sent a sample of clothing that they can comment on. The R&D team then takes the necessary time to analyse these comments thoroughly. The same procedure is also applied to software updates. But the questions are always the same. What are the problems and challenges? What could be better? By involving your best ambassadors in product development, you immediately create the best possible platform for these new products when they are launched. If your ambassadors helped to co-create then, they will certainly be willing to actively recommend them to others.

Of course, what every company really wants is that its ambassadors support its products of their own free will, based on their conviction that the products are good. For this reason, it is important to avoid giving your ambassadors financial rewards or expensive gifts. If someone recommends your product because he expects to get something in return, that is not a genuine recommendation. Instead, it becomes a kind of transaction, and this is no basis for a long-term ambassadorial relationship. In contrast, presenting your ambassadors with modest gifts when they least expect it can help to keep the relationship fresh, spontaneous and credible. Once again, clothing merchandise is a good option. Nothing is more personal than clothing and most of your real fans will be happy to wear it with pride.

In the spring of 2021, Sunday thought that the time had once again come to offer its ambassadors one of their periodic 'treats' in recognition of their efforts. In normal circumstances, it is possible to organise events to which the ambassadors can be invited, but corona meant that an alternative had to be found. Each year, the company brings out its own Spring/Summer collection and Fall/Winter collection of clothing. The theme of the 2021 Spring/Summer collection was Essentials SS21. Normally, these collections are only for internal use as a gesture of thanks to the team, but this time it was suggested by way of a trial to also make the collection available to the company's ambassadors. It was decided to set up an exclusive webshop in which the ambassadors, using a unique coupon code, could order various items of clothing free of charge to be delivered to their home. There was no obligation to order; the company simply wanted to thank the ambassadors for all their hard work.

The online shop was opened at the start of June and everyone employed by the company was allowed to send the coupon codes to anyone who they thought was a true Sunday ambassador. The impact was huge! There were more than a hundred orders on the first day alone. And this was not just because the clothing was free: it was clear that many people were happy to wear the Sunday collection and support 'their' company with pride. But the best was yet to come. When the first parcels were delivered, there was a deluge of posts online from the delighted ambassadors, each one trying to find a more creative way to display and promote the Sunday clothing they had received. In this way, a project that he been organised as a way to express the company's gratitude actually resulted in a massive ROI!

You must ensure that being an ambassador for your company is a fantastic experience. Organise fun interactions with your ambassadors. Keep things light and informal, not stiff and regimented. Never forget that ambassadors are not your employees. They have no obligation to help you; they do so because they want to.

Attract

Attracting ambassadors in a structural manner is the key to growth. There are various potential sources for finding these ambassadors: your own personnel, customers, family, friends, neighbours, suppliers, etc., to name but a few of the more obvious ones. In order to convert someone into an ambassador for your company, you need to take your relationship with that person to a higher level. This takes time and costs energy. However, having a smart ambassador strategy can help to speed up this process.

The very best way to turn someone into an ambassador is to deal with them in a very personal way. This personal approach is always a winner. In this respect, the owner or the CEO of a company can usually have the biggest positive impact. Is that you? If so, you know exactly what you need to do. By conducting personal conversations with potential ambassadors that stress the importance of recommendations, you will motivate them powerfully to make such recommendations. The larger your company, the bigger the challenge, simply because of the number of people involved. Even so, make time each month to talk at a personal level with a number of your team members, customers and suppliers. By explaining your vision to potential ambassadors, you will build up a much stronger connection between them, your company and your brand.

By building the question about whether or not someone is interested in becoming an ambassador into your sales process in a structural manner, you will be able to accelerate the growth in your number of ambassadors significantly. You will find that lots of people are willing to help you grow, simply as a matter of goodwill. Thanking these people sincerely will help you a long way. For this reason, it is a good idea to close a meeting with a new ambassador by saying something like this:

'Thank you for taking the time to talk with us today. As you know, we are a young company and we can use every push in the back that people are kind enough to give us. Do you know other people who might be interested in having the kind of conversation we have just had? If so, please let me know. I would be eternally grateful!'

This is a simple way to show just how much you appreciate the effort that ambassadors make on your behalf. By making structural use of this technique, you will increase the likelihood of finding and converting more and more superfans. And once they start making recommendations, make sure that you monitor them properly and let them know the results in due course.

As a B2C company, it is obviously much easier to conduct individual conversations with every customer and every candidate ambassador. It also makes good sense to have a dedicated landing page on your website that gives additional information about your ambassadorship programme. People can then use this page, for example, to subscribe to an exclusive ambassadors' newsletter. The following points need to be covered on this landing page:

- Why do you work with ambassadors?
- What are the benefits of being an ambassador?
- What can you get by being an ambassador?
- How does your ambassadorial community work?

- What does the company expect of its ambassadors?
- How can you register to become an ambassador?
- What social media channels are used by the company and its ambassadors?
- Testimonies of other ambassadors.
- A clear call to action.

Love

Love is the broadest and most nebulous of the four elements of the DEAL approach.

In his book *Lovemarks*, Kevin Roberts introduced the concept of 'brand love'. According to Roberts, the brands that are truly successful and profitable are not just good brands, but brands with which consumers can build up a loving relationship. But what exactly does this mean? Can brand love be compared with love between people? Or is that taking things too far? It is certainly a question that is worth exploring further.

Brand love

'Love is blind' says the old adage. This applies not only to love between people, but also to the love that some people have for their favourite brand. We have probably all had experience of how Apple, Alfa Romeo or Harley David-son fans react if their love brand is criticised. This reaction is often heated (in some cases that is putting it mildly!) and they are totally unwilling to hear anything bad said about the object of their affection. Research has shown that brand-love consumers become increasingly more loyal as time passes. But it doesn't stop there. They are often also willing to pay more for 'their' brand and to 'forgive' the brand manufacturers if things occasionally go wrong.

What are the characteristics of a love brand? And can this love be measured? The researchers Batra, Ahuvia and Bagozzi[12] conducted a study to try and establish whether or not love for a brand follows the same basic principles as love for a person. The study was in three parts. Two of these parts focused on attempting to identify and map out how people regard and experience love for something other than a person. During this quantitative research test subjects were questioned for between 30 minutes and four hours. Based on the factors in brand love that were most frequently mentioned in these conversations and following a further third study, the researchers developed a model listing the seven most important elements that motivate people to have love for a brand or product.

One of the main conclusions was that a brand lover expects high quality. Because quality is a subjective phenomenon, the researchers interpreted this as meaning that above all the loved product or service should not be the cause of disappointment. This in turn implies that the product or service does not always need to be superior in absolute terms in order to inspire brand love. In fact, a significant majority of the test subjects indicated that they experience a feeling of love for more than one brand.

In light of this basic premise, what are the seven characteristics that most typify brand love? The model developed by Batra, Ahuvia and Bagozzi is as follows:

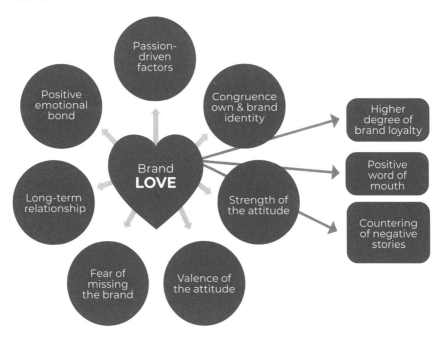

A first component of brand love is a high level of congruence between the respective identities of the brand lover and the brand. In other words, the brand identity says something about your current self-identity or the self-identity you would like to have. Brand love helps to give meaning to your life and provides you with feelings of intrinsic reward.

The second component can be described as passion-driven factors. To demonstrate their brand love, consumers are prepared to invest significant amounts of time and money. In addition, they enjoy using their love brand and have either already been using it for a long time or plan to do so in the future. For example, it is very difficult to persuade an Apple fan to use any smartphone other than an iPhone.

The third component is the existence of a clear and positive emotional connection with the love brand. This can be described as a kind of close friendship with the brand, in a manner that generates positive feelings.

The fourth component is the long-term nature of the relationship with the brand. People who are passionate about a brand are convinced that they are going to be using it for a long time and that it will therefore be a part of their life far into the future.

The fifth component ties in with the previous one and is the fear that brand lovers have of missing their favourite brand, should it no longer exist. For them, the brand is an indispensible part of their existence.

The sixth component is the valence of the lover's attitude towards the brand, its capacity to unite and to promote interaction. Love brands generate relatively strong positive feelings.

The seventh component is the strength of the lover's attitude towards the brand. Brand lovers talk regularly about their brand love and experience few (if any) reasons to doubt the feelings they have for the brand.

Batra, Ahuvia and Bagozzi further concluded that the three most important consequences of brand love are: (1) a higher degree of brand loyalty; (2) positive word of mouth; and (3) the countering of negative stories spread by others. This explains why Apple fans will never hear a bad word spoken about 'their' favourite brand.

Whereas in love between people the participants usually act from unselfish motives – in other words, their behaviour is altruistic – the researchers suggested that this is seldom the case with the brand love. On the contrary, the lovers want to derive 'something' from their brand.

The brand love model offers interesting insights into the nature of the love that people can sometimes have for brands, but it is not always clear how these seven factors can best be stimulated We have suggested some possibilities earlier in the book and a number of matters can certainly be regarded as a kind of 'olympic minimum'. For example, attractive design is one obvious way to appeal to the passion-driven factors and communication can also be geared to place an emphasis on the intrinsic needs of consumers. Equally, brand communities or ambassador platforms can also contribute towards various aspects that will encourage a person's love for a particular product.

Big Green Egg

Big Green Egg is the worldwide number one brand in kamado grills. Their range of Eggs and accessories is available in more than 50 countries and the combination of top design and smart engineering makes it possible to cook almost anything in a simple and relaxing way. The Egg is an icon and a product of undoubted world class. Owning one is making a statement.

Big Green Egg is a brand for which there is a huge amount of brand love. The passion of its superfans is intense and lasting. These superfans call themselves Eggheads and there are numerous official and unofficial forums, Facebook groups and real-life clubs where they meet and share techniques and recipes. Big Green Egg itself also organises 'Flavour Fairs' all around the world. These are truly major events for foodies, with the same allure as the big music festivals, with thousands of fans in attendance.

The company has even developed its own terminology, the use of which helps to bring its ambassadors even closer together. Here are some examples from the Big Green Egg dictionary:

- Egghead: a fanatical user of the Big Green Egg;
- Eggcredible: the moment when your culinary skills reach their highest standard;
- Eggscruciating: the intense pain you feel when you haven't been able to use your Big Green Egg.

Its community of ambassadors is massively important for Big Green Egg. Thanks to their efforts, the brand continues to grow substantially, whilst at the same time retaining the loyalty of its existing users. In fact, the fans' love for the brand is such that Big Green Egg has marketed its own line of clothing for the Eggheads, which is available at its events or via selected retailers.

ACTION POINTS

In this chapter we have discussed various factors that are relevant to the development of an ambassador marketing strategy. Within the DEAL framework, a focus on the pillars of Develop, Engage, Attract and Love will put you on the road to success. The fastest and easiest way to kick-start this process is by circulating your own newsletter to your (potential) ambassadors, making sure you cover the following points:

Develop
- a summary of your products or services, with announcements about new launches;
- an ideal customer story.

Engage
- a summary of your company's vision;
- an explanation of the way the company works.

Attract
- an explanation of why ambassadors are so important for your company, together with a request to find new ones, if possible.

Love
- thank the ambassadors for their support, assure them that their love for your company is mutual and let them see that they are not alone.

Once you have prepared your newsletter, send it to all the people who you regard as ambassadors. If you don't already have one, make a list in Excel or in your CRM system. This will make things easier next time around. Also make sure to stress that the newsletter is 'exclusive' and 'for ambassadors only'. This will increase the likelihood that people will open it.

Monitor the response to your newsletter. When you are contacted by people who have read the letter, ask them what they thought of it. What kind of information would they like to see more of? This gives them a feeling of 'being involved' and will heighten their engagement as ambassadors towards your company.

CHAPTER 6

THE POWER OF MERCHANDISE

MERCHANDISE AS ACCELERATOR

Dress to impress. Clothing determines how we show ourselves to the world. For this reason, the clothes we wear reflect a personal and emotional decision. What things do I like to wear? What brands do I like to wear? With what fashions do I want to associate myself? Clothing is so much more than the body's protection against the natural elements. It is also a primary form of non-verbal communication.

During medieval times, communication was to a large extent something visual. Both in daily life and on the battlefield, people wore specific types of clothing to signal things to each other visually. Striking colours, traditional designs or coats of arms were used to convey important information at a distance. Clothing could also be used to display social status to friend and foe alike. As in almost every other period of history, clothing during the Middle Ages was first and foremost designed to say something about the wearer to others. Comfort and appearance were only secondary matters. Bright colours and rich decoration resulted in a very striking style of dress, especially among the rich, with (to modern eyes) a surprising similarity between the clothes worn by men and women. In general, the more expensive clothes were not distinguished by their design but by the superior cut and quality of the materials used to make them and the ornamentation with which they were decorated. Sometimes, the government of the day intervened to dictate what certain people should wear. For example, some members of the clergy were taken to task because the sumptuous clothing they wore made it hard to distinguish them from the nobility! As today, trends came and went. Sometimes lace-ups were in fashion; just a few years later, exaggeratedly pointed shoes would be back 'in'. Tunics became shorter and shorter as the end of the Middle Ages approached, and it became the height of fashion to show a little more leg... if you were a man![13]

Even in our modern culture, not very much has changed. There are thousands and thousands of contemporary examples of the way in which we still use clothing to show ourselves and what we represent to the outside world. From the scarves of our favourite football team to the t-shirt of our favourite rock band. Branded clothing – or 'merchandise', to give it its proper name – can also make it possible for ambassadors to reach many more people with your message. By providing branded clothing for your fans, you give them tools (which they love wearing!) that can significantly increase your impact.

The questions that companies like Sunday most frequently hear are along the lines of 'Is my brand cool enough for merchandising?' and 'Will people wear my branded clothing if I give it to them?' Many companies have doubts about merchandising and those who tried it in the past often found the experience to be a disappointing one. This was usually because they opted for cheap and poor quality items, which fell apart or lost their colour the first time they were washed. Fortunately, those days are now behind us and modern clothing merchandise is now good enough to be found in quality fashion stores without looking out of place. At the same time, the concept of merchandising has evolved dramatically in recent decades. It now means much more than simply printing your logo on a t-shirt.

If you can choose between an attractive T-shirt of a brand that says nothing to you and an attractive T-shirt of a company in which you genuinely believe, why would you not opt for the merchandise T-shirt? After all, the latter clearly means much more to you than the former. Once they are aware

of this simple fact, few company leaders hesitate any longer to provide their
ambassadors with stylish and high quality merchandise items that serve as
visible tools to increase the company's impact.

MAKING MERCHANDISE A SUCCESS

Because clothing is important to us, we are very fussy when it comes to
choosing it. There are three important ingredients to making sure that your
clothing merchandise is a big success. If you want all your ambassadors to
wear your clothing with pleasure and pride, you need to focus on the quality, the design and the story.

Quality

Nobody likes to be seen in a shapeless piece of material with a print half-fad-
ed from washing. However, this is often the result when price is the only
determining criterion for the company's purchase strategy. In our private
lives, most of us are prepared to pay the right price for the quality of clothes
we want. But when it comes to merchandising for our company, price suddenly becomes the deciding factor. However, this is false economy. If you
buy poor quality clothing merchandise, you are effectively throwing your
money away, because no-one will want to wear it, except perhaps to work in
the garden or to do odd jobs around the house.

Branded clothing can only give you a good return if your ambassadors are
willing to be seen wearing it. If your t-shirts end up in the dustbin because
they shrink or fall to pieces the first time they are washed, you are simply
wasting your ambassador marketing budget. And who is to blame? Not your
ambassadors: they believe in your company so strongly that they want to
promote it with pride to the world, but not with some tatty t-shirt that is
shipped in from South-East Asia by the container load. Investing in better
quality clothing will allow your ambassadors to create a much greater impact, because more of them will be prepared to wear it and they will create
a much better first impression when they do. Remember also that it is the
logo of your brand that is printed on the t-shirt. Do you really want to ruin

years of careful brand development by associating your company name with sub-standard clothing merchandise? Instead of increasing your added value, your reputation and worth will suffer badly.

Weight is no guarantee of quality. This is the most common misunderstanding when people are buying fabrics and clothing: they look only at the weight or grammage, expressed as a number of grams per square metre (GSM) of material. For example, some t-shirts will have 150 GSM, while others might have 200 GSM. But this does not mean that the latter is necessarily 'better' than the former. A lighter 150 GSM t-shirt might sometimes feel more comfortable to wear.

So when you are buying your merchandising, how can you be sure that you are getting the right quality? The best way is to deal with a reliable supplier who communicates clearly. A transparent supply chain also helps to build confidence. These two factors – clear communication and transparency – nearly always go hand in hand with good quality products. In addition, it is also a good idea to always work with pre-shrunk materials. These fabrics will already have been washed before the t-shirt or sweatshirt was made, which should avoid unpleasant surprises when your ambassadors first throw them into the washing machine (providing they set the right temperature!). Some cheap promotion brands deliberately steer clear of pre-shrunk materials for budgetary reasons, because the shrinkage results in less fabric, which means that in comparison with 'normal' fabric you need more of it to make the same number of t-shirts. In general, however, it pays to opt for pre-shrunk.

Another factor that can no longer be overlooked when talking about the clothing industry is whether the working conditions of those who are employed in it are ethical. No self-respecting company can allow its merchandising products to be manufactured in the appalling working conditions that are still found in some parts of the world. Fortunately, there are a number of alternatives for textile production that are more transparent in this respect, which explains why Sunday has deliberately chosen to work exclusively with a family-run company in Europe (Poland). This makes the situation much easier to monitor and control, and allows both partners to grow together through a process of constructive dialogue and mutual respect. Initiatives such as Fair Wear also help to bring about further positive evolutions in the textile world. Based on its series of independent and thorough inspection visits, the Fair Wear Foundation awards a quality label to companies with exemplary working practices.

Sustainable entrepreneurship also means paying due attention to ecological matters. Like working conditions, this is another important societal factor that companies ignore at their peril. Many companies in the clothing industry are now taking steps to reduce the size of their ecological footprint and many of the industry's customers are applying the same principle to the clothing merchandise they buy. In recent years, this has resulted in a number of interesting evolutions, such as the increasing use of organic cotton or alternative fibres like tencel or seacell.[14] At the same time, a number of technological processes have been developed to increase the recycling of textiles, so that a wide range of recycled cotton is now available. Similarly, technology has also created a number of new synthetic materials, such as those that can be made from plastic bottles. These trends are expanding year by year and Sunday has decided that it wants to play a pioneering role in this process. By focusing on the use of ecological, recyclable and recycled materials, the company is able to offer an additional benefit to its customers. Nowadays, a sustainable label is a plus point for any merchandising product.

'I love it when a plan comes together.'

Hannibal, The A-Team

Pittman Seafood

A great example of a perfect blend between ecology, storytelling and customer objectives is the merchandising products that Sunday developed for Pittman Seafood, an important player in the wholesale fish distribution industry. The company attaches great importance to sustainable entrepreneurship and respect for the oceans, and wanted these ecological objectives to be clearly reflected in its merchandising. With this in mind, the creative department at Sunday came up with the idea of fun socks, decorated with a pattern of fish and lobsters. Nothing special, you might think?

But the truly unique aspect of the project was the fact that all the socks were made using recycled fish nets! In this way, the company was not only provided with socks that were eye-catching and cool to wear, but also had a direct link through the material with the company's mission and vision of the future.

Design

The design of merchandise is another important factor that will determine whether or not your ambassadors will be willing to wear or use your merchandising products. This is an area where many companies get it wrong. Far too often they wish to put far too much information on their garments. We have all seen (or been given) t-shirts with a massive logo on the front and all the relevant company details on the back. Can you still visualise that t-shirt?

And can you still recall any of the data on the back: website, e-mail address, phone and fax numbers, etc.? Did you ever send them a mail? Or give them a call? No, we thought not.

If you want to develop a clothing line for your brand, you need to take three factors into account: your target public, current fashion trends and (of course) your own house style. The challenge for the designer is to combine these three elements in a balanced way that results in attractive and wearable clothes. Understanding your target public is particularly important: if they like your clothing, they will wear it; if they don't like it, they won't. You also need to decide what you want them to wear and when. Depending on your events and objectives, do you need t-shirts and sweatshirts, or something a bit more formal? Clothing for the teambuilding of a hip tech start-up will look very different from the trade fair 'uniform' used by a service company. By taking account of your target group and the prevailing circumstances, you will increase the likelihood that your merchandising will actually be worn.

In this respect, taking current fashions into account is essential. Your clothing merchandise will need to stand in comparison to all the other items of clothing in your ambassador's wardrobe! This means that you will need to keep abreast of what is happening in the fashion world. What styles and colours are currently 'in'? Which ones are 'out'? The more closely your clothing merchandise resembles trends in the real world, the more your ambassadors will love it – and wear it! At the same time, responding to the latest trends in this way emphasises that your company is alert, up-to-date and relevant.

Fashion trends are also important in helping to determine the choice of merchandising products. For example, a few years ago snapbacks were all the rage. These are the American baseball-style caps with a large front peak and a plastic clip fastener at the back, which owed their initial popularity to their appearance in the hip-hop scene. A short while later, the trend became mainstream, so that hundreds of companies were suddenly ditching their ordinary merchandising caps in favour of this new 'underground' model, with its much cooler image. In the meantime, this particular hype has died down, because that is the nature of hypes: they come and they go. But you can always count on a new one to emerge sooner or later. So be on the look-out!

Fashion trends also differ significantly from country to country. Sunday's country manager in The Netherlands always finds it amusing that Belgian companies so often seem to order grey t-shirts, whereas Dutch companies think grey looks awful and nearly always opt for much brighter colours. For this reason, it can be quite a challenge to design clothing merchandise for international companies that will be accepted in all the different cultures where they operate.

Taking account of your target public and fashion trends is a good start, but you still need to link your merchandising to your company. As already mentioned, this requires much more than just printing your logo on a t-shirt. Your logo is just one feature of your house style and you need your company clothing to reflect all aspects of this house style as closely as possible. Use the right pantone colours, so that your pullovers have the same sky-blue that features in your company crest. Or add an amusing insider joke to the washing label as an extra special touch. Designing merchandise means designing the whole product, not just its superficial characteristics.

At companies like Sunday, designers are busy every day combining the above three elements to create unique and, above all, wearable clothing for customers and their ambassadors. If you want to be as certain as you can that your merchandising products will be appreciated and worn, you are well advised to work with a supplier that has plenty of experience in designing clothes of this kind. It really is specialist work, and they can guide you through all aspects of the process, not only indicating what is technically possible, but also what is affordable.

Sint Bernardus

Sint Bernardus (St. Bernard) is a well-known Belgian brewery that has been making beer for more than 120 years. One of its most popular brews is their St. Bernardus Abt (Abbot), which helps to attract beer enthusiasts by the coachload to the brewery's Experience Centre in Watou. After the recent and successful development of this centre and its guided tours, it was time to pay attention to the adjoining shop. Every marketeer knows that a good physical customer journey should always end in a shop. And after such a journey in a brewery, which visitor would not be interested in sampling and buying some excellent beer?

Sint Bernardus realised early on that the power of merchandising could help to turn these visitors into true ambassadors. Every tourist or local who wore a Sint Bernardus pullover would automatically be a walking advertising board for the brewery and its products.

When developing its merchandising theme, the brewery was faced with two options:

Option A: cheap promotional gadgets and clothing sold at low prices.

Option B: a good quality line of clothing that people would be happy and proud to wear, and for which they would be willing to pay a premium price.

Initially, Sint Bernardus – like so many others before them – went for the first, cheaper option. However, the results were disappointing. Not only were sales lower than expected, but nobody was interested in continuing to wear clothing that was clearly cheap and shoddy.

In consequence, the merchandise was failing in its twin tasks of increasing the brewery's name recognition and building up a community around its brand. Faced with this unsatisfactory situation, Sint Bernardus belatedly decided to change course and switched to the second option: better quality clothing that nobody would be embarrassed to wear.

It was a smart move. The new clothing line was an instant success, with some items repeatedly sold out. Just as importantly, the brewery started to receive dozens of social media posts showing Sint Bernardus superfans wearing their pullovers, scarves, etc. at home and amongst friends, which has given a significant boost both to the visibility of the brewery and the sale of its beer. The most loyal of these fans now form an ambassadorial community online. Mission accomplished!

© shop.sintbernardus.be

Story

You can increase the likelihood that people will want to wear your clothing merchandise by building up a strong story around it. Without doing anything to change your products, you can increase their value simply by offering people the emotional experience known as 'unboxing'.

The popularity of unboxing videos illustrates the importance of the moment when someone receives a present, parcel or gift and underlines that this moment is an important part of the total product experience.

Compare the following two scenarios.

In the first scenario, you are working in your office when you receive the following mail.

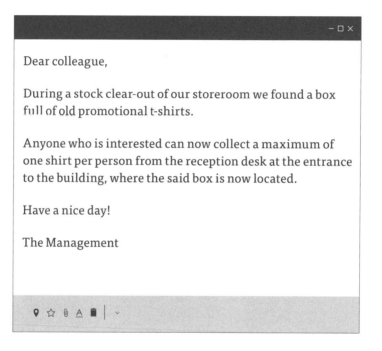

Dear colleague,

During a stock clear-out of our storeroom we found a box full of old promotional t-shirts.

Anyone who is interested can now collect a maximum of one shirt per person from the reception desk at the entrance to the building, where the said box is now located.

Have a nice day!

The Management

As an enthusiastic employee, you go and have a look at the box when you are leaving for home that evening. You find that it is packed full to overflowing with crumpled t-shirts, most of which your colleagues have already rummaged through more than once. You think about trying to find one in your size that has not already been unpacked and handled, but eventually you decide to give it a miss...

This is a classic example of how not to do things. Neither the communication nor the experience are stimulating, so that the value of the merchandise is reduced. If people actually bother to take a t-shirt, they have been given no real reason to wear it, except perhaps when they are doing a painting job at home. You might as well have just thrown the shirts in the rubbish skip.

Same office, same t-shirts, but the following scenario is completely different.

You arrive at the office and walk up the stairs to your room, having first wished your colleagues a friendly 'good morning'. When you get to your desk, you are surprised to see a neat package resting on your keyboard. The box completely matches the branding of your company: same colour, same typeface, etc. On the box you read the single word 'Congratulations!' As you slowly start to open the package, your heart begins to beat just a little bit faster. Inside the box you discover a perfectly folded t-shirt and a handwritten note explaining what it is and why it is on your desk.

Hello Nicolas,

Congratulations! It is your company birthday!

You have been our much liked and much valued colleague for the past five years!

We are delighted to offer you this t-shirt as a small token of our appreciation of all the hard work you do for the company.

Wear it with pride. You have earned it! Have a great day!

The Management

While the t-shirt is identical in both scenarios, the story and the unboxing in the second scenario provide an experience with a significantly greater value. As a result, there is actually a much greater likelihood that you will wear the t-shirt. This illustrates just how important it is as a company to think carefully about how you can improve the total experience of your merchandising products. You can compare it with the dressing of a plate for a meal: the better the presentation, the more people will appreciate the quality of your cooking.

Mobile Vikings: Something wrong? That sucks!

Mobile Vikings is a Belgian virtual mobile phone operator that is well known for its amusing adverts and jingles, which seem to appeal to young and old alike. Mobile Vikings targets its messages primarily at users, who are interested in mobile surfing as often as possible and as long as possible for as little as possible. Thanks to the company's no-nonsense approach and a regular series of interesting special offers, Mobile Vikings is mega-popular with mobile data lovers!

One of the main USPs of Mobile Vikings is their super-fast help desk. The company is available 24/7 to assist customers with all their problems and queries. In this way, Mobile Vikings seeks to provide its users with a real 'wow' experience whenever they need to call for help, cementing them still further into the brand community. This community feeling is one of the keys to Mobile Vikings' success. To emphasise the feeling, the company refers to its customers as 'Vikings', which increases their sense of involvement and makes them feel part of the Mobile Vikings family.

To underline this 'family' approach, Mobile Vikings regularly sends all its Vikings small gifts, to remind them and to prove to them that they are all equally important to the company. Many of these gifts have a humorous slant and nothing encourages word of mouth better than sharing something funny. People just love to make each other laugh!

As part of its clever marketing strategy, Mobile Vikings makes use of hats and socks as customer gifts. In this context, they talk of 'happy surprises' or 'sad surprises'. Because the Vikings are the true ambassadors of Mobile Vikings, the company wants to make happy Vikings even happier by sending them a happy surprise. If, however, something happens to make a Viking less than happy, the company then sends him/her a sad surprise, which is a pair of socks with the text: 'Something wrong? That socks!' Hilarious, don't you think? In this way, the situation is defused with humour and the customer is once again encouraged to see Mobile Vikings in a positive light.

© Sunday

HubSpot

HubSpot is a well-known American company that develops marketing, sales and service software that helps companies to grow. It is the reference at world level for inbound marketing and was largely responsible for putting this form of marketing on the map. Since HubSpot was founded in 2005, it has attracted no fewer than 114,000 customers worldwide. To establish and maintain a close connection with these customers, the company makes use of account-based marketing or ABM.

The traditional marketing and sales funnel is based on leads entering the funnel at the top and then following a path of awareness until a purchase is completed. This is a very broad approach based on volume. You need to cram as many leads into the funnel as you can, in the hope that enough of them will emerge at the bottom to make your business viable.

With account-based marketing, the sales funnel is turned upside down as part of a more targeted approach, based on carefully selected customer accounts. Instead of trying to catch fish with a big net, ABM uses a rod and line, but with the right bait. And, like many other companies who have adopted the ABM philosophy, with success.

Once of the main differences between ABM and traditional marketing is that ABM places a much stronger focus on people as individuals. In other words, they think carefully about who they really want to make ambassadors for their company.

For this reason, HubSpot concentrates many of its marketing efforts (unique marketing actions) on individual customers instead of opting for mass communication. They do this with great care and skill, and their aim is to build up genuine connections with their customers at important moments in their lives. With this in mind, they have developed a complete range of HubSpot clothing, which their account managers can send to customers in whom they believe to mark appropriate life events. For example, there are bibs and romper suits for customers who have just become parents or cool track suits for those who are known to be interested in sport.

By devoting special attention to these key moments in the lives of their ambassadors, a closer bond with the company is forged that results in more positive communication about HubSpot.

The essence

To close this section, it is well worth repeating the essential factors that will allow you to develop successful clothing merchandise products. It is crucial – repeat, crucial – to take into account the quality of the clothing, the stylishness of its design and the total experience it creates when it is presented to or discovered by your ambassadors. If you bear these three factors in mind when taking decisions about your branded clothing, you will soon be rewarded by seeing your team members, customers and other stakeholders proudly wearing your merchandise garments, resulting in a tighter bond with the wearers and greater visibility amongst those who are yet to discover your company.

ACTION POINTS

The fastest way to set up a successful merchandising campaign is to choose the right partner company to work with. The following five steps will show you how to achieve an immediate ROI from your ambassadors through the use of merchandise products.

To demonstrate these five steps, we will use a fictitious company as an example: Anne's Florist Shop. Anne is known above all for her fabulous floral creations for weddings.

- Determine your budget and your objective. Travelling without having a destination in mind is pointless. What do you wish to achieve and how much can you spend to make it happen?

Anne's objective is to provide and arrange all the plants and flowers for five new weddings. To make this possible, Anne is prepared to allocate a marketing budget of 1,000 euros.

- Decide which ambassadors you can use to help you achieve your objective (your personnel, best customers, family, friends, etc.). Who are these people and, above all, what merchandise articles do you think they would wear with pride?

Anne's best ambassadors are married couples for whose weddings she has already supplied brilliant floral displays. She decides to try to activate 25 of these couples through merchandising.

- Choose a good merchandise partner and work together to devise/develop a product that you think will help you towards your goal. Think about the total experience that people will get when they receive the product.

Anne chooses Sunday as a partner (of course!) and agrees with them to make 25 sets of 'his and hers' slippers, which will be presented in unique packaging that makes the message she wishes to convey crystal clear.

- Make a plan for the successful distribution of your merchandising. Most merchandising campaigns end their days in a dark cupboard at the back of a warehouse or storeroom. Devise clever ways to ensure that your merchandise products will be fully used.

Anne builds a presentation moment into the wedding day itself. She presents the slippers to the happy couple during the reception, so that they can take them with them on honeymoon. To make sure that she never forgets the slippers, she keeps two pairs in each of her company's vehicles.

- Follow the progress of your campaign and measure its impact in figures. This is the only way to know in black and white whether or not your venture into merchandising has brought sufficient ROI to be a success.

Four weeks after each wedding Anne organises an evaluation moment with the married couples. Were they satisfied with everything? What was the honeymoon like? At the end of the session, she refers to the slippers and explains that small companies like hers rely heavily on recommendations, if they wish to grow. If they know of other couples who are planning to marry, Anne and her team would love to provide the flowers. As they were so happy themselves, perhaps they could recommend Anne for the task?

If you follow these five steps in all your merchandising campaigns, you will cover all the factors that you need to cover and will be in a position afterwards to know precisely what ROI you have achieved.

EPILOGUE

Hopefully, *Create Your Own Superfans* will have given you clear insight into how ambassador marketing works. Every manager and business leader knows the power of recommendations. They are a very effective way of increasing your turnover and of gathering people around your company to form a community. The more people you have in this community, the stronger your company will become.

This book was a journey through the theory and practice of ambassador marketing. The numerous examples from various sectors all illustrate the same point: if you want your company to grow in a healthy and sustainable manner, you need the help of loyal ambassadors. Finding them is by no means as hard as you might think. People have a natural reflex to form into 'tribes'. Our entire social system is built upon the foundation of people coming together in groups that are stronger than the individual. This survival strategy, which has existed since primeval times, is also the starting point for ambassador marketing. Because we all attach such importance to the opinions of the members of our 'tribe', these people are able to influence our choices.

This theory has been confirmed by countless independent research studies, which have demonstrated beyond doubt that recommendations are viewed by consumers as being more reliable than any other marketing channel. This alone is reason enough for entrepreneurs or marketeers to include ambassadorship in their marketing strategy. Throughout all these studies, no other research question has even shown such a clear correlation with potential growth as the question about whether or not someone would be prepared to recommend your company.

Whether you are talking about attracting new customers or recruiting new members for your team, ambassadorship can have a powerful influence on people who are contemplating an association with your company. In each of the awareness, consideration and decision phases, your ambassadors can play different roles. By understanding these different roles, you can develop a strategy that allows you to use the ambassadors in the right way at the right time.

If you only take away one thing from this book, let it be this: whether you are a small independent entrepreneur or the global marketing director of a huge multinational, ambassador marketing is the very best way to guarantee growth. You need to invest time and money in building up an army of ambassadors, because they are the people most capable of pushing your company forwards, both in the short term and in the long term. So remember the golden rule: never be too afraid or too embarrassed to ask for a recommendation. You won't regret it.

ACKNOWLEDGEMENTS

About a year has passed since I had my first conversation with Stefan about this book.

After this conversation, I threw myself wholeheartedly into the project, with just a single goal in mind: to get the book written. It was difficult for me to assess what this might involve, what problems and obstacles I might meet along the way, but I had a clear mission to make one of my childhood dreams come true. I now know that writing a book is a rollercoaster ride. It forces you to bring together all the loose fragments of thought floating around inside your head, so that you can form them into a clear and structured unity. It was a wonderful experience. The more we worked together on the book and its various chapters, the clearer everything seemed to become.

First and foremost, I would like to thank my partner Zymcke for always believing in me. She was even more confident than I was that I would eventually bring this project to a successful conclusion. She helped me to find calm when I was too hard on myself and was hard on me when I started to let things slide. In addition, she also kept our wonderful and energetic young daughter Olivia lovingly occupied during the hundreds of hours that I needed to devote to my writing. I would also like to thank Olivia as well. Without knowing it, she was the best possible motivation to see things through to the finish. I hope that she will one day read this book with pride.

My deep gratitude also goes to my partner Steven Calles. Without him, there would be no Sunday. What started out as a loose exchange of ideas on a Monday evening in a bar in Roeselare later developed into the most important source for all the experience and knowledge contained in this book. In addition to Steven, I would also like to thank the entire Sunday team. In their different ways, they have all had an impact. A special mention goes to Karel-Jan Vercruysse for our long brainstorming sessions about ambassadorship, the DEAL framework and so much more. And also to Daniel Wójcikowski, the man who taught me the true meaning of the words 'We'll manage' and without whose passion we would not be standing where we are today. Last but not least, there is also Céderic Veryser, a man on whom I can always rely. His many efforts on my behalf allowed me to find the necessary mental space to write this book.

I would also like to thank my parents, Kathleen and Joost, who have always been there for me. When I used to tell them about my great life dreams as a child, they always offered me their unconditional support and gave me the proverbial 'wings' that I needed to reach my goals. My grandfather Marcel has also been a great source of inspiration. It was he who showed me how you can make your own future. He must have told me a hundred times about the way he built up his own impressive career, even though he left school at the age of fourteen. My grandmother Klara taught me that discipline and continuity are the best ingredients for achieving great things, while Uncle John was always willing to be my sounding board and was also the man who first introduced me to Stefan all those years ago.

Of course, I must also thank my entire family for being the truest of true ambassadors for me.

I cannot not finish without expressing my deep and heartfelt thanks to Stefan Doutreluingne for his collaboration on this project. His expertise and experience were crucial. What began as a wild idea a year ago has finally ended up as this book. Thank you, Stefan, for making it the most marvellous experience.

Niels

ENDNOTES

1   Van den Bergh, J. & Behrer, M. (2014). *How cool brands stay hot*. Leuven: LannooCampus.
2   Warren, C. & Campbell, M.C. (2014), What makes things cool? How autonomy influences perceptions of coolness. *Journal of Consumer Research*, 41(2), 543-563.
3   Conick, H. (2018). How to win friends and influence millions, the rules of influencer marketing. Via https://www.ama.org/marketing-news/ how-to-win-friends-and-influence-millions-the-rules-of-influencer-marketing/
4   Digimeter 2020 – Imec.
5   UBA Belgium – Media Key Facts 19-04-21.
6   Brightlocal_Local Consumer Review Survey 2020.
7   Weber Shandwick Aankoop & Beslissingsproces Belgische en Europese consumenten.
8   Medium.com: how Zara survives with minimal advertising – Postfun- nel. com
9   Nielsen Global Trust in Advertising Report 2018. 10 https://www.makersmark.com/ambassadors
10 https://makersmark.com/ambassadors
11 https://ideas.lego.com
12 Batra, R., Ahuvia, A. & Bagozzi, R.P. (2012). Brand love. *Journal of Marketing*, 76(2), 1-16.
13 Coss, P. (2012). *Heraldry, Pageantry and Social Display in Medieval England*. Suffolk: Boydell Press.
14 Tencel is a fibre made from the ground pulp of eucalyptus. Seacell is a fibre made from seaweed.